IT FEELS BETTER WHEN I LAUGH

A merry heart doeth good like a medicine:
but a broken spirit drieth the bones.
(Proverbs 17:22)

IT FEELS BETTER WHEN I LAUGH

RICK CORAM

FOREWORD BY JUNIOR HILL

ANEKO PRESS

Visit Rick's website: www.rickcoramministries.com

It Feels Better When I Laugh – Rick Coram

Copyright © 2017

First edition published 2004

Scripture quotations are from the King James Version of the Bible

Cover Illustration and Design: Natalia Hawthorne, BookCoverLabs.com

eBook: Icons Vector/Shutterstock

Editors: Sheila Wilkinson

Printed in the United States of America

Aneko Press – *Our Readers Matter*™

www.anekopress.com

Aneko Press, Life Sentence Publishing, and our logos are trademarks of

Life Sentence Publishing, Inc.
203 E. Birch Street
P.O. Box 652
Abbotsford, WI 54405

RELIGION / Christian Life / Inspirational

Paperback ISBN: 978-1-62245-519-5

Hardcover ISBN: 978-1-62245-521-8

eBook ISBN: 978-1-62245-520-1

10 9 8 7 6 5 4 3 2 1

Available where books are sold

Contents

To Judy
My wife, friend, and ministry mate. You have blessed my life with your unending encouragement and support. You are the best. Thank you for always leaving the front porch light burning! I love you.

To Rachel, Jessica, and Jonathan
You are my three gifts from God. I have not always been around, and yet you have been so understanding about the ministry that God has chosen for us. Thank you for sharing your daddy with so many others. I love you.

Foreword

Rick Coram is one of the best preachers in America! I have been listening to him speak for many years and am always blessed by his passionate delivery of God's Word. But in addition to his fervent speaking style, he is uniquely and delightfully funny. He is able to use personal illustrations, many of them from his own life and ministry, to teach humorous but spiritually applicable truths.

In this delightful book, *It Feels Better When I Laugh*, you will find stories, which will bless your heart as well as tickle your funny bone. In a day of constant bad news, it is encouraging to have something pleasant and uplifting to read. I sincerely believe readers will be blessed by this brief treatise from one of the most delightful and heart-stirring preachers of our day.

Junior Hill
Evangelist
Hartselle, Alabama

Preface

I spend most of my life on the road. At times it seems that there is an endless cycle of airports, hotels, restaurants, and rental cars. The weeks often run together, and there have been some days that I have awakened and had to stop and think for a moment exactly where I am. Now, please don't misunderstand me. I am certainly not complaining. God has placed the wonderful call of evangelism on my life. That means I get to travel from place to place, sharing the glorious gospel of our Lord Jesus Christ! But there are seasons of the year that the length of the highway and the loneliness of the hotel rooms can take their toll.

God has blessed me with a wonderful family. My wife Judy and my three children (Rachel, Jessica, and Jonathan) are the joy of my life. The two girls were both very young when God called me from the pastorate to full-time vocational evangelism. Our son was born only one year after I became a traveling preacher. That means that all of his life he has watched his daddy pack a suitcase and leave home. Many times when he is stepping up to bat or dribbling a basketball down the court, I am stepping into the pulpit to preach another message. I have missed some very important home runs and jump shots over the years. Now, he seems to understand why Dad is not always there. When he was ten years old, I asked, "Son, do you resent the fact that Dad can't be at all of your games?" He innocently looked at me and said, "No sir, you are busy telling people about Jesus." God has richly blessed me with a family who both understands and supports His call on my life. He has also reminded me to enjoy each and every moment that I can be at home.

But I must confess there have been times that I have felt sorry for myself. There have been days that I have allowed the enemy to throw a *pity party* for me. Of course, the only two who were at the party were the devil and I! One of those sad parties occurred in a lonely hotel room several years ago. The reason I am telling you about it now is because of something simple that happened to cancel the party. God used the gift of **laughter** to encourage me and actually place on my heart the reason to write this book. This is what happened: I was preaching a revival in a dead church. On top of that, I was physically tired and at the end of a long series of engagements.

I had already missed several of my son's baseball games, and on that Tuesday night, I had missed a game in which he hit a big home run. After calling home that evening and hearing the news, at first I was excited for Jonathan. But when I hung up the phone, a great spirit of despondency overwhelmed me. As I sat in that chair, I thought about the dead service I had just preached in.

I thought about how much I would have loved to see my son hit his home run, and how I could never recall that moment!

Suddenly the enemy began to attack me. In my spirit he said things such as, *You sure are a lousy dad! And you are a failure as an evangelist! Here you are in a church that doesn't care enough to come to revival, and you missed another one of your son's games!* Well, I listened to him until he had completely defeated me. I stayed in that chair until I was a limp wimp. The devil worked me over and turned me every way but loose. After what seemed like hours (In reality it was about fifteen minutes), I slowly got up, loosened my tie, and began to change clothes. Tears were actually streaming down my face as I considered what a failure I was, both as a preacher and a father. Finally, as I pathetically fell back down in the chair of despair, I reached over to pick up the newspaper I had bought earlier in the day. Strictly by force of habit, I opened it and began to look. I don't think I really intended to seriously read that paper. Actually, I was kind of numb, and I was just glancing. Then, quickly it happened – I spotted a simple little cartoon located on the editorial page. It was a cute, clean, carefree, small cartoon tucked away on the bottom of the newspaper, but it was absolutely hilarious. I smiled, then I chuckled, and the more I thought about it, I began to laugh out loud. In fact, I laughed until it felt good. As I sat there and smiled, I thought about the promise found in God's Word.

Proverbs 17:22 says, *A merry heart doeth good like a medicine: but a broken spirit drieth the bones.* The word *medicine* in the Hebrew language means "something that promotes healing." That simply means that a merry heart is God's medicine for the soul. Have you ever noticed how good you feel when you laugh? The medical community agrees that it is important to laugh. A doctor who wrote a book on health said that happy emotions affect the pituitary gland. That gland then secretes chemicals that are distributed to the entire body.

When you laugh, it helps you relax and release tension. When you laugh, it serves as a statement to the enemy that you will not be controlled by your circumstances. When you laugh, it is good medicine to clean your heart, cure your health, and clear your head.

That night I discovered once again that the devil is a liar and that my God is faithful. It is amazing how God used a small little cartoon to help get my attention. Of course that cartoon had no spiritual power, but laughter is a powerful healer. After I had that good laugh, something significant took place. I realized how utterly foolish it was to let the devil discourage me. God had so abundantly blessed me! I slipped to my knees and thanked God for my family. I thanked Him for giving my son health to play baseball. I thanked Him for the way He had blessed my life and ministry. There were so many things to thank Him for that I started laughing for joy because of His goodness. When I went to bed that night, I fell asleep realizing that I was a victor and not a victim. I was reminded that Nehemiah was correct when he said, *For the joy of the Lord is your strength* (Nehemiah 8:10). I was again reminded of the words of Proverbs 15:15 that say, *All the days of the afflicted are evil: but he that is of a **merry heart** hath a continual feast.* There is a healing medicine that comes with a heart that is happy. And a good dose of laughter is always healthy. Laughter is good therapy for the soul.

Perhaps your heart needs a good dose of laughter today. I pray that something in this simple little book will help. This is not a book of jokes, quips, or anecdotes. It is a book that records some interesting real life things that have happened to me on the evangelistic trail. After all, the really amusing moments are those that we get ourselves into. The funniest things in life are the ones that happen to us. And sometimes nobody but God is looking!

Life is a journey, and sometimes it is not funny. But when we can look back and laugh about some of our situations, it is good for us. And when we can learn a spiritual lesson, it is even better. So come take this journey with me, and I hope that it blesses you. I have discovered one important thing on this journey – the trip is not always easy, but *It Feels Better When I Laugh!*

Because Jesus Lives,
Evangelist Rick Coram
Jacksonville, Florida

Chapter 1

Hawg Huntin'

Immokalee, Florida, is a small town located in south-west Florida, about thirty miles from the Gulf of Mexico. It is famous for growing beautiful tomatoes, cucumbers, and sugar cane. It is also noted for its wildlife. I got close to some of that wildlife during a revival meeting at the First Baptist Church of Immokalee. The pastor had two teenage boys who introduced me to hawg huntin'. No, that is not a misspelling. The first lesson I had to learn was proper pronunciation. It is not hog hunting; it is hawg huntin'. Now, I am not much of a hunter. As a boy, I was raised up fishing the freshwater lakes of Florida.

However, I agreed to go hog hunting (excuse me, hawg huntin') with them. So, after revival service one night, they picked me up in the truck. I noticed that the pickup truck was full of dogs. These dogs are called hawg dawgs. There were several other young men from the church, but there were no guns. I soon discovered that in Immokalee they didn't hunt hawgs with guns. We drove out into the woods, and they began to shine bright lights out into those palmetto bushes. Soon they had scurried up a hawg. Now these are pretty fierce looking creatures. They are big and they have two wicked looking tusks sticking out. These things are mean and mad. We aren't talking about the three little pigs here. As the hawg began to run, the boys turned loose the hawg dawgs.

The first dawg to reach the hawg opened his mouth and grabbed him by the ear. That hawg thrashed around and swung that dawg from side to side. But I want you to know that faithful dawg hung on like grim death. After a period of time, that hawg began to wear out, and then the most amazing thing happened.

One of those teenage boys hollered, "It's my turn!" And with that he jumped down out of the truck and ran over to the hawg. He sat on the hawg's back and pried the dawg's teeth loose from off the hawg. Then he began to slap the hawg! Finally, the boy jumped up and started sprinting back to the pickup truck. Well, let me tell you, that hawg was mad. After all, he had had a dawg on his ear and a boy on his back! At first, you could tell that the hawg was a bit confused. But as soon as he got his bearings, he came running after that boy.

Now, it was about fifty yards back to the truck. With that mad, ear-pierced hawg chasing him, the boy was racing as hard as he could for the bed of that truck. All of his buddies were cheering for him. The young man dove into the back of that pickup like a baseball player sliding head first into a base. That hawg was so mad that he put his head down and slammed into the side of that Ford truck. The truck was actually rocking back and forth, while those boys were whooping and hollering to one another.

As I watched those boys giving each other high-fives and chest-bumping one another, I was absolutely amazed at their sheer delight. I remember thinking, "You guys really do need to get out a little more!" But do you know what happened to me? As the evening wore on, my attitude changed completely. I got caught up in all of the excitement. Before it was over, I was cheering for them. Truthfully, I really wanted to let a hawg chase me. Thankfully, the pastor wouldn't let me do it. After my sanity returned, I realized it was a wise decision. After all, it could really hurt the revival if a hawg speared the traveling evangelist.

Nevertheless, I stayed in the back of that truck and exchanged high-fives, chest-bumps, and congratulations. And I must admit, it was really kind of exhilarating. When I returned to my room that night, I phoned my wife Judy. She asked me why it took me so long to call, and I shouted, "I went hawg huntin' tonight!" She burst out in laughter.

Later, I realized how ridiculous that statement was. I didn't go hawg huntin'. I didn't sit on a hawg or let a hawg chase me. Why, I didn't even get out of the truck! Truthfully, I was really just a hawg huntin' spectator. I didn't physically exert myself, but I certainly did cheer on the ones who were doing the hunting.

Sadly, that sounds a great deal like the modern day church. It seems that many congregations have more spectators than servants. Almost everywhere I go, pastors seem to be lamenting the fact that so many of their members are uncommitted. Most churches are always crying for more workers. There never seems to be enough help in the nursery or with children or with teenagers. I know of a church with over five hundred members that had to cancel Vacation Bible School. The reason was simply that there were not enough volunteers to adequately supply the school.

Many of our churches have plenty of people in the pews, but it appears that all they are doing is watching. It looks like a lot of Christians are cheering on the singers, the preachers, and the workers, but they themselves are watching from the truck. There is a lot of applause and cheering coming from the bench. But there seems to be fewer people in the game. There are a lot of soldiers in the army, but it doesn't look like that many are in the battle.

We are living in a generation that is accustomed to being entertained. Unfortunately, that same attitude has drifted into the church. It has spawned an era of Christianity that is puzzling indeed. There are a lot of professing Christians who will drive a hundred miles on a Saturday night to cheer at a gospel concert. Yet they will not drive ten miles on a Sunday morning to serve God in their local church. Others will collect books and tapes of great preaching. They will be moved by the messages they hear but not motivated enough to get busy for God. It seems that more saints would rather sit and soak than stand and serve. Far too many believers would rather watch than work.

In Romans 1:1 Paul declared himself to be a *servant of Jesus Christ.* The word *servant* is the Greek word that means "bond slave." In those days it was a serious matter to be a bond slave. It was a lifetime commitment. In fact, a ceremony was held in which the bond slave made his commitment public. The slave would kneel in the doorway of his master's house. He would then lay his head up against the doorpost. Someone would take a hammer and an awl, and punch a hole in the earlobe of the slave. The hole was big enough to run a pencil through. It signified that the slave was marked for life. He was the property of his master, and he would serve that master with all of his heart, soul, and body. That is what it means to be a *servant* of Jesus Christ! It is serious business, and we should be willing to serve our Master with an absolute, unrivaled surrender. That kind of surrender is not one that sits idly by and looks on while others labor.

Do you remember the ultimatum that Jesus gave the huge crowd who was following Him? Thousands were walking behind Jesus as He traveled. They cheered His miracles and marveled at everything Christ said and did. But in Mark 8:34 the Lord turned to them and said, *Whosoever will come after me, let him **deny** himself, and take up his cross, and follow me.* After He said those words, the crowds got smaller and smaller. Finally, there was only one disciple who stuck it out all the way to the death of Jesus. There were a lot of people who had watched the show. Plenty of them experienced goose bumps and thrills. Many of them applauded and cheered. But they were nowhere to be found when it really counted.

I heard the story of the great revival that swept through a country church. One night they were having a testimony meeting. It was exciting to hear. A man stood up and proclaimed, "I've been drinking, but God has gotten a hold of me, and I'm going to quit it!"

When the saints heard him, they shouted and cheered, "Hallelujah, that's revival!"

Another man stood and said, "I've been stealing, but God has gotten a hold of me, and I'm going to quit it!"

Once again there was loud affirmation and applause, and the folks shouted, "Hallelujah, that's revival!"

This went on and on throughout the evening. There was one confession after another. People were vowing to quit this or that. At last, there was a little old lady sitting there who really was not guilty of any terrible sin. But she got caught up in the excitement and wanted to participate. She leaped to her feet and bellowed, "I ain't been doing anything, but God has gotten a hold of me, and I am going to quit it!"

Friends, there are a lot of Christians who don't seem to be doing anything for God. It is time for them to quit it and start doing something! When that happens, it will be revival. We have too many who seem to be watching from the back of the truck. The time has come to go huntin'!

To every thing there is a season, and a time to every purpose under the heaven ... A time to weep, and a time to laugh (Ecclesiastes 3:1, 4).

Blessed are ye that weep now: for ye shall laugh (Luke 6:21b).

Chapter 2

Running For a Drink

Life on the road is very demanding. There is nothing routine about the daily schedule of a traveling evangelist. Mealtimes will vary from church to church, but one thing is certain; there is always plenty of food. Whether you are taken to a fine restaurant or dine in a home, people always want to be sure that the evangelist is well fed. When I leave most churches, I can honestly say that I am a *full gospel preacher*! On top of all that, the preaching and travel can interrupt proper sleeping habits. So, it is easy to see how an evangelist can have a lifestyle that can become unhealthy.

I had been a traveling evangelist for only one year when I realized that I was not getting proper exercise. Since I had been a sprinter in high school, I decided to take up jogging. In a moment of utter stupidity, I determined that I would begin jogging three miles a day! After purchasing some running shoes, I started out on this exciting new adventure. Well, the thrill lasted for about two days.

I had barely staggered through one mile per day. That is when I came to the conclusion that this may well be the most boring sport in history. Think about it: you always stop in the same place you start. In addition to that, you see the same sights, and the same dogs chase you at the same locations! And so, I just stopped jogging. Then I began to feel guilty because I had not followed through with my commitment.

At the time we were living near Jacksonville, Florida. One day I read in the Jacksonville newspaper that the River Run was coming up that weekend. I read about thousands of runners who were going to compete in this race that would cover 3.1 miles. I also read that anyone could sign up and run. Immediately I thought, "This is just what I need!" After all, we all need a goal to motivate us, and the competition would be exciting. Now, bear in mind that I had yet to complete one mile, let alone three! But nevertheless, I went out and bought myself a sharp runner's outfit and got set for the River Run!

Saturday morning dawned bright and clear and very warm. There I was with thousands of runners loosening up before the big race. About that time some official stood up on a platform and spoke into the microphone. He asked, "How many rookie runners are here today?" I proudly raised my hand along with many others. He continued, "Be sure to hydrate yourselves. This Florida sun will wear you out. Be certain that you have properly hydrated your body with plenty of liquids." When he finished, I saw many runners quickly go over to the table and fill up with water or Gatorade. Of course I did not go over and drink anything. After all, I used to run in high school, and I reasoned that I was still a bit of an athlete. I mean, this wasn't the Boston Marathon we were talking about here! It is only three little miles! I concluded that I had hydrated myself before I left home, and I will hydrate when I get back home.

After the water break, all the runners got back in place, and the race began. I started real slow because I wanted to pace myself. Unfortunately, I looked up and realized that I was in dead last place. Even all of the senior adults were ahead of me. It was at that point that my male competitive ego kicked in and I began to sprint. Here I was, racing past people like some Olympian. In my mind I could hear the song, "Chariots Of Fire"! Well, that lasted for about two hundred yards. At that point I was pretty well worn out. As I approached the one-mile mark, my rapid pace eventually slowed to a stagger. When I arrived at the marker, I was happy to no longer be in last place. However, it was painfully obvious to me that the next two miles would be difficult.

With great agony I continued jogging, walking, and almost crawling to the two mile mark. There was a pole erected to represent the distance of two miles. I completely stopped for a moment to hang onto that pole and try to motivate my aching feet to trudge on. There I was, saturated with fatigue and literally expecting my heart to explode. I'll be the first to admit that what happened next was stupid and silly, but I confess that it's true. Incredibly, I began to talk to my shoes! I said, "I hate you shoes! When I get home, I am going to burn you! If I can just make it back, I will never run again!" I would have quit right then, but I realized that it would be easier to go one mile to the finish than go back two miles to the start.

In any case, I left the pole and began that last excruciating mile. Every time my weary feet hit the asphalt, it felt like fire shooting up though the rubber soles of those hated shoes. Each small stride seemed as though I were running in place and the finish line appeared to be moving away from me. Suddenly I looked down on the pavement and saw the number, *2.5 miles.*

The end was really close now! That is when a sixty-five-year-old woman (she later told me her age) effortlessly glided past me. She flashed a sweet grandmotherly smile and waved her hand. As I was gasping for breath, she said, "Keep on going son, you're going to make it!" I can't tell you how pathetically worthless I felt as I watched this precious white-haired woman, thirty years older than me, blow past me!

Now, experiencing total humility, I summoned up my last ounce of strength. I remember thinking, "It's not happening today, grandma! I will not lose to you!" Straining and sucking wind, I was able to find a little motivation. I want you to know that I caught that sweet granny, and I smoked her by two yards at the finish line!

After finishing the race, I really thought I was going to die. My family walked over to love and encourage me, but I had one thing on my mind. I needed to get a drink. Over at the water table I loaded up with water and juice. Pouring that refreshing liquid on me and in me, I gulped it down and then went back for more. My wife Judy escorted me over to the edge of the St. Johns River, and I sat down under a beautiful tree and rested.

It wasn't long until the cool breeze from the river and the gentle rustle of that shade tree began to soothe me. My daughters brought me more water, and some of the other runners, including that precious sixty-five-year-old woman, came over to encourage me.

Twenty minutes later I was walking to my car. Judy looked at me and asked, "How was it?"

I looked back at her and replied, "I enjoyed that so much, I think I will do it again!" That is amazing isn't it? In the middle of the race, I felt like quitting. I did not think that it was worth the effort. But after being refreshed with water, I knew that the race was worth running.

Have you noticed that some of God's greatest warriors often get battle fatigue? Some of the most determined runners seem to stop in the middle of the race. Many of them quit running because they never get a drink. Remember that it is very important to stay refreshed. If you don't, you will drop out of the race. There is a clear example of that in the Bible. Check out what happened to Samson in Judges 15:14-20. Those verses describe the great achievement of God's warrior killing a thousand men. But be sure to examine carefully what happened after the battle. Judges 15:18 says, *And he was sore athirst.* The word *athirst* means that he was totally depleted. Samson had won a great victory for God. He was not *defeated,* but he was *depleted.* He was physically, emotionally, mentally, and spiritually worn out. The battle had been won but Samson was whipped.

The Scripture goes on to tell us that because he was worn out, he lost his faith. Samson got filled with pride, and then he began to pout. Judges 15:19 explains: *But*

God clave a hollow place that was in the jaw, and there came water thereout; and when he had drunk, his spirit came again, and he revived.

All of us who are saved are running in a race. God reminds us of that fact in His Word. *So run, that ye may obtain* (1 Corinthians 9:24). We are on the track team of the Trinity. Our race is not a sprint, it is a marathon. Be sure that you get a drink along the way. Don't forget your daily time of refreshment in God's Word. Take a moment to stop and pray for daily filling. Hydrate yourself with a holy drink from the river that never runs dry.

Chapter 3

Keep the Snake Out

I am in that populous category of folks who hate snakes. We believe that the only good snake is a dead snake. I love the story I heard of the country pastor. Someone asked him, "Preacher, do you believe in handling snakes?"

The pastor answered back, "Yes sir, I believe in shovel handling them."

Amen! I certainly agree with that preacher. In fact, my fear of snakes is so real that I won't even handle one of the rubber ones at Wal-Mart.

Wouldn't it be a terrible thing if a snake got in the house? Not too many years ago that very thing almost happened to the Coram house. I happened to be home that hot Florida summer day, and I had just finished eating lunch. There were errands to run that afternoon, so I got up from the table and headed to the front door. My youngest daughter Jessica was playing near the doorway, and I stopped to tell her goodbye. Judy walked me to the door. As I opened it and stepped outside, my wife let out a bloodcurdling scream and quickly slammed the door. Don't ask me how I knew, but I just knew that her scream was a snake scream. Without stopping to look, I jumped straight off the porch and out onto the yard. Then I looked back and witnessed the most amazing sight. There was a huge blacksnake standing erect on my porch! Now, this is not some fictional tale that I am trying to get you to believe. It is the absolute truth.

Actually, it is very easy to explain. We were in the process of remodeling, so our front porch stoop was only temporary. It was made of wood, and there were small gaps between the sections. That big snake was lying inches from our front door. Well, when I walked out, I stepped on his tail. My foot pressed his tail down inside one of those gapped spaces, and he shot straight up in the air. Imagine the sight that Judy beheld.

Here she is opening the door, and instantly a five- or six-foot snake rises up in her face! Then, as I turned around, I saw something that was just as strange. The snake was literally standing up and as he tried to free himself, he was gyrating back and forth! Naturally I was looking for the nearest way to get on the roof and out of his way. At the same moment Judy was peering out the side window. Through the glass she was trying to explain to me why she had so abruptly shut the door. She didn't need to bother; I was looking at the evidence right in front of me. Then, that wicked looking serpent wiggled free, plopped down on the ground, and swiftly slithered around the corner. I watched him slide through the grass and out into the woods behind the house.

As soon as Judy realized he was gone, she opened up

the door. She looked at me and explained, "Sorry dear, but I wasn't about to let that snake get in the house. Our daughter was right here by the door. I didn't want that snake to get near her."

I responded and told her how much I appreciated her care for our little girl. And then I had to remind her, "But you left me outside with the snake!"

It certainly would save a lot of heartache if parents would be that aggressive in locking the enemy out of our homes. Revelation 12:9 calls the devil *the serpent which deceiveth the whole world.* He is the snake who wants to crawl into homes and destroy our families. In Genesis chapter 2, Adam and Eve got married. Then in the very first verse in Genesis 3, the serpent shows up to destroy them. The very first institution that the devil ever attacked was the family. In Genesis 3:13, Eve told God, *The serpent beguiled me, and I did eat.* The Hebrew word *beguiled* means "to mentally seduce." That is exactly what the snake is doing to the homes of America. He crawls in and attacks the minds of our families. Be sure to guard your television and your computer. Be certain to lock your doors to books and magazines that can corrupt your children. Listen, my friend, the snake managed to poison the perfect family living in the perfect culture. If he could do it to them, then he can surely do the same to your family. Wise up parents – don't let the snake in the house!

Chapter 4

Speaking of Snakes

My home state of Florida is a very beautiful state. It is a state with a variety of landscapes. You will find everything from palms to pines to palmettos. We have farmland, swampland, and sandy beaches. In one part of our state, you can find tropical plants; and in Ocala, Florida, (where I live) you can find sprawling horse ranches. Florida is a kaleidoscope of lakes, streams, rivers, oceans, marshes, and forests. Why, we even have some rolling hills. And in all of this magnificent landscape, you can find plenty of snakes. Lizards without legs, that's what I call them. They thrive and survive in the humid climate of Florida.

So, you would think that one of the best places to find a large snakeskin in a closet would be in a house in Florida. But I found an extra large snakeskin in a beautiful home in the mountains of West Virginia. When I first became a traveling evangelist, I wanted to be accommodating, so I decided to stay in homes rather than hotels. That lasted for about a year. Not only is it difficult to rest and study, it also places a strain on the daily schedule of the family that is keeping me. In addition to that, I ran into one or two weird experiences. One of those occurred in West Virginia during my first few months on the road.

Upon arriving at this home, I was ushered upstairs to my bedroom. I have this one small quirk when it comes to suitcases. Once I reach my destination, I want to go ahead and unpack my entire luggage. It makes me feel a little more at home I guess. In any case, I was placing my shoes down in the closet when I noticed something against the baseboard on the back wall.

As soon as I picked it up, I shuddered. It was a snake-skin, and there was plenty of it! A short time later, I sat down at dinner with the delightful family I was staying with. I told the man of the house that I had found the skin in my room. He said, "Oh yeah, we got us a big old blacksnake running around here somewhere. We see him from time to time. He's a big one, but he won't hurt you." As I was choking on my food, he continued, "He catches rats and bugs. He's like a member of the family. We believe he lives in the attic above your room." Needless to say, I had lost my appetite. First of all, here I was staying with a family who considered a snake a relative; second, he had the apartment right over my head! Third, the problem was not the snake hurting me, the problem was me seeing the snake and hurting myself!

Now, this was only Saturday night. That meant that I had to be in that house until the revival ended on Wednesday. Paranoia sank its ugly teeth into my mind and took over. For the next four days I expected to see that snake. Every time I awoke, I halfway believed that I would see him lying on the dresser, or on the floor, or on top of me! After all, he might come back for his skin.

Finally, Thursday morning arrived, and the pastor came to take me to the airport. As I was closing my luggage, I double-checked to make sure nothing extra was in my suitcase. (I think you know what mean.) Well, when I at last sat down in that pastor's car, I can't tell you the relief that overwhelmed me. It was finally over; I wouldn't have to live in the same place as that snake anymore!

It doesn't take a rocket scientist to see that we are living in the same world as the devil. Check the newspaper or watch the news on television, and you will agree. The wicked old snake has poisoned and perverted this planet. He has wrapped himself around our generation and is squeezing it to death. Imagine how absolutely liberating it will be when we don't have to live in the same place as the devil. Do you realize that you have never lived in a world without the devil? Cheer up, child of God, because that day is coming! Revelation 20:10 clearly says, *And the devil that deceived them was cast into a lake of fire and brimstone, where the beast and the false prophet are, and shall be tormented day and night forever and ever.* Hallelujah, the saved are going to the land that is fairer than day, and the devil is going to the lake of fire! And for the first time in our lives, we will live in a world without the devil. Come quickly Lord Jesus.

Chapter 5

Enjoy the Trip Home

Florida is a great place to live. As I travel the country, it is funny to hear some of the questions people ask about Florida. The most amusing questions come from those who have never been to my home state. For example, I can remember one year when the annual Southern Baptist Convention was going to be held in Orlando. Several months before the convention, I was preaching a revival meeting in the state of North Carolina. One morning that week, I was invited to speak to the pastors of that area. It was one those breakfast gatherings, and it was very informal. Surprisingly, a few of the pastors had never been to Florida, and the convention was going to be their first visit. When I was introduced as a resident of Florida, I was asked some very unusual things. One man was concerned about alligators, and another had heard that hardly anyone in Florida spoke English.

Well, I decided to have some fun. I told them, "Be careful where you drive, because alligators will come right up and bite your car tires." Then I told them, "It would be good to take a crash course in Spanish, or you won't even be able to order dinner." Needless to say, it didn't take long for them to realize that I was pulling their legs. However, there was one fellow who still wasn't sure about the alligators. He had come to pastor in North Carolina from somewhere out west. Because he had never been to Florida, the poor man had some misconceptions about my state. He really thought that once you cross the Florida state line, you would see monstrous gators roaming the interstate highways. He also believed that most everyone in Florida had come by boat and was speaking a foreign language.

And I am quite sure that he was fearful of sinking into a murky swamp or at least of being eaten by gigantic mosquitos! Hopefully, when he came to Orlando, he discovered that some parts of Florida are actually nice to visit.

Speaking of visiting Orlando, Florida, that reminds me of a delightful story. Much of the time I fly out of the Orlando International Airport. No matter where I fly to, one thing is certain. The flight back to Orlando will almost always be packed with families and children. They are either headed for a cruise ship in Port Canaveral, or they are going on vacation to one of the theme parks that central Florida is famous for. Well, whatever their final destination, you can count on one thing. The flight to Orlando is always eventful. That airplane is alive with the sound of children. But I can remember one morning when the noise started even before we boarded the plane.

I was on one those early bird flights out of Raleigh,

North Carolina. I had gotten to bed late after our final revival service. The irritating wake-up call had come far too early at about 3:00 a.m. Now it was 6:00 a.m. as I made the walk down to my gate. After I fell down in my seat at the gate area, I looked around at the other people who were sitting there. It suddenly occurred to me that these folks looked as if they felt as miserable as I did. Sitting across from me was a well-dressed business man. The expression on his face told me all that I needed to know about his attitude. To my right was a guy who was close to falling asleep and dropping his hot coffee. On my left was a dear woman who had already drifted off into some pretty serious slumber. She sounded as if she were snoring in about five different languages. As I continued to survey the scene across that room, I took note of something. There was not one person in that gate area that looked happy. Every countenance was grim. Nobody looked content, carefree, or happy.

Then, like a string of firecrackers exploding, here they came. You could actually hear them before you could see them. I swiveled my head slowly around and saw where the noise was coming from. It was roaring out of about six or seven small packages. The packages were in the form of little children. These live wires were running down the corridor and being chased by two frantic women. Naturally, they were coming to our gate. And brother, let me tell you, they woke up the entire area.

Instantly, they raced over to the window and pressed their smiling faces to the glass. When they spotted the huge jet at the gate, they turned up the decibels! One little boy spread his arms and pretended to be a 747. A pretty little girl let out a piercing yell of delight. All of the kids were either running, screaming, climbing, or standing on chairs. Meanwhile, the two exhausted mothers looked like they were going to cry. I am telling you, it appeared that these ecstatic children had eaten chocolate eggs for breakfast along with sugar-coated pancakes. In the middle of it all, one young boy came running over to me. Why he picked me out, I will never know. Nonetheless, he got right in my face and said, "Hey, mister, wanna know where we're going! We are going to Disney World!" Then he spread his arms and ran back over to the window. He pointed out to the airplane and blurted, "And that big plane is gonna take us!"

One of the women spoke to me and apologized, "I'm sorry sir. He is so excited." Then she added, "I don't know which thing these kids are more excited about – Disney World or the airplane ride to get there."

I looked at her and smiled, "Oh that's all right; it is good to see somebody that is happy at this time of the morning."

After getting on that airplane, I began to think about what that woman had said to me. What she was really saying was *these kids aren't just looking forward to the destination. They are thrilled with the journey.* I want you to think about that for a moment. If you are saved, you are certainly looking forward to heaven. The Bible makes it clear that this world is not our home. First Peter 2:11 reminds us that we are *strangers and pilgrims.* A *stranger* is someone who is away from home, and a *pilgrim* is someone who is on the way home. God is preparing a place for us that is absolutely unimaginable. Every single believer should be anticipating that glorious day when we are taken home.

But we must also remember that we are not home yet. Sadly, I am afraid there are far too many Christians who miss out on the joy of the journey. They spend so much time expecting heaven tomorrow that they are not enjoying heaven today. They are so busy looking for heaven that they are not living for heaven. We all need to be reminded that heaven is waiting. But let's remember to count and caress the blessings that we are given today. Some people miss a blessing because they never recognize it. I love the fantastic story of Joseph and his brothers.

Even after they had sold him into slavery, he loved them and wanted to bless them. God elevated Joseph to a lofty position of power, and He used him to save his brothers from famine. After his brothers repented, Joseph told them that he wanted them to come live with him. Then he helped his brothers prepare for the long journey to his house. Genesis 45:21 is a wonderful reminder of the Christian life. That verse says, *Joseph gave them provision for the way.* That is exactly what our Lord has done for us. He promised to provide for us on every step of our long journey home. Even when the trip gets hard, He has given His word that He will give us what we need. Unfortunately, there are some days when I spend so much time griping, I fail to see His glory. I fail to recognize another miracle He has bestowed upon me.

Philippians 4:11 says, *Not that I speak in respect of want: for I have learned, in whatsoever state I am, therewith to be content.* Do you know where the apostle Paul was when he wrote this verse? He was living in a small room, chained to a Roman soldier, and he was subsisting on a small diet. However, none of those things affected his contentment. He depended on his heavenly Father for all things. He determined that his chief duty in life was to enjoy and glorify God. As I travel down the road, I am excited about my future home. But I surely do want to enjoy the trip there. After all, this old world will be the only hell that I will ever see!

Chapter 6

God Is My Pilot

As I write this particular chapter, I am sitting in a Delta jet that is climbing at about 20,000 feet. It is a Saturday night flight, and I am on my way to Greenville, South Carolina. While looking out the window at the lights below, I thought about all of the miles I have flown. As you can imagine, I have had a few unusual experiences on airplanes.

Once I was on a small plane that was taking a short trip from Atlanta en route to Chattanooga. That flight was also a night flight, but it was a nasty night. Violent thunderstorms had delayed us for two hours. Now, as we took off, there were still storms in the area. Our flight reached its cruising altitude and then it got interesting. Flashing lights suddenly began to light up the inside of the cabin. People started screaming all throughout the plane. Then there was another flash, quickly followed by yet another. For a moment, I really thought the plane was on fire. The entire inside of that dark jet was shining. It was then that the captain told us what was happening. He said, "Ladies and gentlemen, we are flying through a storm. The light you have just seen has come from lightning. Please stay in your seats with your seatbelts fastened."

I looked out of my window at a truly awesome sight. One bolt of lightning after another pierced the nighttime sky. It was so powerful that it continued to literally light up the inside of that airplane. Sitting next to me was a woman who was visibly shaken. She looked at me and asked, "Do you fly much?"

I replied, "Yes ma'am, I do quite a bit of traveling."

Then she wanted to know, "Is this normal?" I told her that I had never flown in a storm this bad, but at the same time I reassured her that we were going to be safe. Of course I was trying to reassure myself as well! Then she asked me what I did for a living. When I stated, "I am an evangelist," she started smiling.

"Oh good," she exclaimed, "God is not going to let a preacher die!" Well, I tried to explain to her that if it was time for us to go, my being a preacher wouldn't make a difference! But it did give me a wonderful witnessing opportunity.

* * * *

Flying presents some interesting ways to share your faith. There was another time I was seated by a lady who was intrigued by my vocation. I was reading over my message for Sunday morning, and I had my Bible lying on the seat tray. The woman looked over, saw the Bible, and smugly said, "I am a very educated person, and I do not believe that there is a God." I shared with her how Jesus Christ had changed my life.

She seemed to listen intently as I described how real my God is to me. After I had finished, she argued about all the disasters in the world. Of course her conclusion was, "How can there be a God? If He were really alive, then all the misery in this world would not exist."

Once again the opportunity was there for me tell her about sin and its destructive effect on our planet. I lovingly told her how the blood of Jesus washes away sin and makes us new creations. Politely, she once again sat patiently until I was through speaking. Then this lady told me her pedigree. Very proudly, she recited her multiple college degrees. Her demeanor was cool and confident as she listed the schools she had attended and the brilliant authors she had read. She was certain there was no God. Obviously, I had done all that I could do.

We must remember that we cannot *argue* someone into repentance. Unsaved people cannot be talked into conversion. We do not have to try to prove anything. God has commanded us to be faithful and diligent in telling a lost world that Jesus saves. But it is God alone who gives the increase. Salvation is a matter of the heart, and it must come by faith. So, it was apparent that I was speaking to an avowed agnostic, and the agnostic wasn't budging.

But it was absolutely astounding what happened several minutes later. Without warning, we hit some unexpected turbulence. And this was not your average, run-of-the-mill turbulence. This was one of those bottom-falling-out types of turbulence. That jet suddenly began to feel like a roller coaster. Well, when it happened, the agnostic I was sitting beside got frightened. Do you know what she yelled out? That agnostic shouted, "Oh God we're going down!"

When it became apparent we weren't going to crash, she quickly recovered. The woman looked at me with a sheepish, embarrassed expression. I just sort of smiled. What I wanted to say was, "Who was that you were just talking too when you thought you were dying?" But I tried to remain humble. It was interesting to me that she was certain there was no God. Yet His name was the first one she called out when the bottom started to drop.

* * * *

Back in the 1970s a bumper sticker was introduced. It was a catchy little phrase that said, "God Is My Co-Pilot." Now, that might sound cute when you first say it. However, the truth is this: God is not *co* anything. My sovereign, supreme, supernatural God does not need any help. He is the one who is in control. Our lives and existence are literally in His hands.

I thought about that a few years ago when I was scheduled to take a US Airways flight out of Charlotte, North Carolina. As we got prepared to board the plane, it was announced that there was a small "mechanical" problem. We were assured the wait would be minimal because they were swiftly working to correct it.

Then, after another half hour, the attendant at the gate spoke again. She said, "Ladies and gentlemen, we are sorry for the delay. But the cockpit window is cracked. It is being repaired, and we will have you on your way as soon as possible." The passengers at the gate area were not excited about the news. First, there was anger over the delay, but there was also consternation about a cracked window.

I walked over to the desk and asked the attendant, "Is there perhaps another plane that could be substituted?"

She sweetly told me, "No, because Charlotte is a US Airways hub, all of the available planes were in use." We waited another half hour, and people were really upset. To calm the discontent, the woman spoke once more, "Once again we apologize for the inconvenience. It has taken this long because they wanted to replace the entire window." Then she proceeded, "However, after they removed the window, they discovered no new one was in stock. It looked as if we were going to have to cancel the flight altogether, but they were able to put the window back in and repair it. The plane is on its way back to the gate."

I could not help but think that maybe she wasn't supposed to tell us all of that. Her employers may not have wanted people to know about the lack of supplies in the stockroom. Also, her explanation did little to pacify the passengers. Business people had missed meetings, and others had missed connections.

As the griping continued, we watched from the big window as our plane was wheeled back into place. There was no doubt that they had worked on the window. We could all see the construction done on the left side of the cockpit glass. One man spoke up and asked, "What is that gray stuff?"

Another man quickly answered, "I don't believe it! That is Duct Tape!" It wasn't very reassuring to know that we were about to fly on a plane that would be traveling at 500 miles per hour, and the only thing holding the cockpit glass together was good old Duct Tape.

As we prepared to board, the young woman took the microphone to make one more announcement. She said, "Thank you for patience. All alcoholic beverages will be served today at no cost." For the first time all afternoon there was applause and cheers. I boarded the plane that was held together by Duct Tape. No alcoholic drink was necessary for me. I was secure in the fact that my Father had everything under control. His hand holds a lot tighter than Duct Tape!

* * * *

It is still incredible to me how those huge, heavy airplanes ever get off the ground. Flying is one of mankind's greatest achievements. Yet, I am constantly reminded that the most modern jets are still just mechanical equipment, and mechanical equipment sometimes fails. Someone has said that an airplane is really nothing more than a metal tube filled with explosive jet fuel. And that tube is hurtling through the air at hundreds of miles per hour! Somehow, that is not too comforting. But in reality, it is true.

One day I was flying on a Delta jet that was headed to Atlanta, Georgia. I am a frequent Delta flyer, and that means that I make many connections in the Delta hub of Atlanta. Hartsfield Airport in Atlanta is one of the busiest and biggest airports in America. I have spent countless, weary hours waiting there. Because of that, I know the place pretty well. In fact, I could probably tell you what restaurants are located in each concourse.

On this day however, I was awfully glad to set foot in that airport. As our big jumbo jet was preparing to land, everything appeared to be normal. It was a cloudless, beautiful spring day. I looked out the window and saw buildings and sights that I was very familiar with. We descended over the massive Ford assembly plant. I knew that meant we were about to touch down. It always seems as though we are going to scrape the roof of that building when we land from that direction. Then, right before we felt the wheels hit the runway, the captain pulled back the throttle, and we took off. With a rush we began to steadily climb again. I want you to know, there was a rush in the cabin as well. What in the world was going on? Passengers exchanged puzzled glances as we once again circled high above the Atlanta skyline. Then we began to move away from Atlanta. Now we were flying over Stone Mountain, away from the airport!

At last, our captain spoke to us about what was happening. His explanation was not exactly what we wanted to hear. He said, "You are probably wondering why we didn't land. As our landing gear was lowered, we received no indication that it was locked into place. We believe that it is a simple malfunction of the indicator light, but we must take precaution. It has taken a few minutes to get back into the landing pattern."

Then he paused and told us this, "Now ladies and gentlemen, as we land, you may see some unusual things. They have foamed the runway just in case. You may see some emergency and rescue vehicles on the sides of the runway. I don't believe any of that will be needed. I believe this is a simple light malfunction. I am confident our gear is fine. Please do not be alarmed."

Let me tell you, his words did not have a calming effect on the passengers. The man in front of me exclaimed, "Oh no, oh no!" People were tense and you could feel it.

Now, I am a man who loves God and walks by faith. And at that second, my faith was doing a few flip-flops. You see, I am excited about going to heaven. I also know that my steps are ordered, and my days are numbered. But I was thinking about my family, and how I sure did want to see them again! Suddenly, we were back over that Ford plant. All of us braced as those wheels touched down. As soon as it was obvious that the landing gear had locked, people broke out in spontaneous cheers. There was more celebration on that airplane than I see in some Baptist churches on Sunday. The worried man in front of me turned to his wife and gleefully said, "See, I told you we would make it!"

Everybody laughed and clapped as she disdainfully looked back at him and loudly said, "Oh, shut up, you big baby!'

* * * *

One day I was returning home from a revival in Kansas City, Missouri. And once again I had to connect in Atlanta before returning to Orlando. About forty-five minutes into the flight our captain said, "Ladies and gentlemen, we have a 170 mph tailwind behind us." The captain continued his warning by saying, "When we begin our approach into Atlanta, we are going to encounter some very rough air." Then, about fifteen minutes later he spoke to us again. He reminded us, "We are preparing to descend out of this tailwind, and I want to urge the flight attendants to please finish cabin service." A few minutes later he made one more announcement. He told the flight attendants to sit down, and he told the passengers to be sure we were seated and buckled up. Once more he mentioned the rough air. It wasn't long after that until the big jet began to dance about the sky. The turbulence was extremely rough as we bounced downward toward Atlanta. From my vantage point I could see the right wing move up and down as if it was a large bird flapping its wings. As we continued our descent, the choppiness did not decrease. It was about that time that we hit an air pocket. With an audible thud and jerk, that plane fell through the altitude. It was worse than I had experienced in a long time.

I was sitting next to a very pleasant couple. The lady was sitting in the middle, and her husband was right next to the aisle. He grabbed the hand of his wife and actually said, "I must confess, I am a little scared."

She tried to soothe her husband and quietly said, "Just trust the pilot, he will get us there." I was amazed how serene and calm this confident woman was. Truthfully, I was mildly flustered by the whole ordeal. In fact, I kind of wanted to squeeze her other hand and let her reassure me!

After we safely landed, I waited until everyone had departed. I knew that I had a bit of a layover, and others had close connections. So, I literally was the last one to get off the plane. As I got to the door, the pilot and co-pilot were exiting the cockpit. I thanked them for a safe flight. The co-pilot smiled, and then he pointed to the pilot and said, "You were in good hands. He is the best."

When I was a sixteen-year-old boy, I trusted Jesus Christ as my Savior. It was at that moment that I got on board the flight headed to heaven. My pilot promised me He would get me there. In Ephesians 4:30 the Word says, *I am sealed unto the day of redemption.* That word *sealed* means that I am "secured and preserved." Now, my pilot didn't promise me the sky would always be clear. He did not tell me that there would never be turbulence and storms. But He did promise to keep me and carry me.

As I told you before, I am writing this on a flight to Greenville. The seatbelt sign just came on. It feels like the air is getting a little rough. Oh well, there is no need to be alarmed. I have confidence in the pilot.

> *It is of the Lord's mercies that we are not consumed, because his compassions fail not. They are new every morning: great is thy faithfulness* (Lamentations 3:22-23).

Chapter 7

Tithers or Tippers?

Someone has said that the most sensitive nerve in a man's body is that long one that runs from his ear to his wallet. That seems to be true when it comes to tithing. Some church members actually get red-neck mad when the pastor preaches about stewardship. Of course, those are usually the very ones who are not committed to tithe. They are the people who believe that the same twenty-dollar bill that is too small for the shopping mall is too much for the offering plate. Sadly, far too many professing Christians have that stingy attitude. People who give with that kind of spirit are tippers, not tithers. After they have taken care of everything else, they tip God a little bit once in a while.

Well, after leaving the pastorate, my personal commitment to tithing was put to the test. For the first time in my ministry, I thought about becoming a tipper. Here is how it happened: Several months after stepping into full-time evangelism, the money well was beginning to run dry. Pastors were not exactly knocking down my door with invitations for revivals. After all of these years, it is overwhelming how God has abundantly filled my calendar with places to preach. My gracious Father has provided so many invitations that they cannot all be filled. The calendar is booked with engagements that are over two years into the future! It is still all a bit mind-boggling to me, and I never take it for granted. It is always a serious and high honor to stand in any pastor's pulpit. But in those early days, we were excited if the calendar was booked for one month. Our tight ministry budget struggled to operate from week to week. There were not any extra funds to work with. Over these years, God has provided our ministry with some generous, faithful supporters. Month in and month out, they consistently help meet the needs we face.

However, there were very few of those people in the early days. So, we solely depended on the love offerings that came from revival meetings. And, in that first year, there was not a full slate of revival dates. During my first four months in this new adventure, there were some great pastor friends who booked me. But when those ten or eleven engagements were over, the pace was painstakingly slow. Suddenly, I examined my calendar and noticed a lot of empty space. Three months down the line there were plenty of dates, but I only had two opportunities to preach until then.

One of those opportunities was a small, one-day revival. On the Friday before that event, I did what I did every week. Without fail, Judy or I would write the tithe check that would go to our local church. Since early in our marriage, we have given God first place in our family budget. With deep conviction we have acknowledged that God is the owner of everything. I believe the Book from cover to cover, and the Book says, *Bring ye all the tithes into the storehouse* (Malachi 3:10). And so, after entering traveling evangelism, Judy and I continued to tithe without reservation or hesitation. There was never a question about it. That is, until the bank account bottomed out. I discovered all of that on that particular Friday when I got out the calculator and did a little math. We had exhausted most of our savings in setting up the evangelism ministry. It had been several weeks since I had received a love offering. Needless to say, the calculator showed me a bottom line that I did not want to see. I came to the sober realization that if I wrote that tithe check there would be next to nothing left in the checkbook. Common sense demanded that I just put the checkbook away – so I did. After all, I simply reasoned that I could always catch up the tithe a little later. But as soon as that checkbook hit the desk drawer, the Holy Spirit hit my heart. God reminded me that vocational evangelism is a walk of faith. He told me to keep doing what I had committed to do. My heavenly Father gently reminded me that He would supply our every need.

I knew in my heart that I needed to tithe and then trust the Lord. And so, I took out the checkbook and prepared to once again write that check. But instead of faith, all that I saw were figures – bank figures – and those figures were pitifully small. So, instead of writing the tithe check, I decided to negotiate with God. You know what I mean, don't you? I felt like I needed to bring God up to speed on my situation. I wanted to be sure that He was completely aware of exactly where I was!

Oh, I am sure that you have never done that, but I eloquently explained to Jehovah Jireh why I could not tithe this week. Satisfied with my decision, I once again dropped the checkbook in the drawer and left the room. But alas, my personal satisfaction was superficial, and it was only temporary. In just a few minutes, guilt began to grip my heart. I was absolutely miserable. God turned me every way but loose.

Walking back over to the desk, I reluctantly pulled out the checkbook and dutifully wrote out the tithe. Suffice to say, I was not very hilarious about it. To be perfectly honest, I was a little bitter about the whole thing. I remember murmuring something under my breath. As I recall, it went about like this: "If I had more revivals, then I would have more money to give!" If these tight-wad Baptists would give to me, then I could give more to you!" Well, I finished the check, put it in the tithing envelope, and left the room. It was all ready for Judy to drop in the offering plate on Sunday. I would be on my way to the one-day revival. I think you will agree that I was not in real tip-top spiritual shape to preach, but what happened on that Sunday, I will never forget.

Early on that Lord's Day, I traveled about four hours down to Central Florida. The church that I was preaching at had a congregation of about 250 people. Upon my arrival, I was stunned to see that the pastor was out of town! He was at Ridgecrest on a retreat. The pastor had booked me to come, but he never told me that he wouldn't be there. He called it a one-day revival, but in reality I was really just the "pulpit-supply preacher." Now, there is nothing wrong with being a "supply" preacher. There are many wonderful preachers who are able to step in when the pastor is away. But I was counting on this being a big day in my infant evangelism ministry. So, I just did something that is easy to do when you function in the flesh – I began to gripe. I let the devil convince me that I had made a tragic mistake in ever leaving the pastorate. Here I was, in a relatively dead church. On top of that, an ill-informed staff member was in charge of my love offering. All I was likely to get was an honorarium for gas. I would in all likelihood have to pay for my hotel for the afternoon. Then it hit me – I didn't have enough money, because I tithed! Now let me ask you a question. Aren't you glad you were not there to hear the message that Sunday? I don't remember what it was, but it had to be pathetic. It was coming from a disillusioned, discouraged, dry evangelist.

During the worship service, I sat and seethed on the front row. As I had suspected, nothing was said to the congregation about my love offering. Now, as you read this, please don't be too shocked at my honesty. I am just telling you the truth. I was messed up and mired in the quicksand of self. My enemy was running roughshod on me. Later a chilling thought occurred to me. Aren't you glad that God doesn't publicly deal with us like He did Ananias and Sapphira when we get selfish? The great evangelist Vance Havner had something to say about that. Dr. Havner said, "If God dealt with us like He did Ananias and Sapphira, there wouldn't be enough ambulances to haul the corpses away from the church!" As for me, all of my priorities were misplaced, and I was more concerned about money than I was about ministry.

Yet, in spite of me, God poured out His blessings. When the invitation was concluded, I was asked to go stand at the door and shake hands with the congregation. I trudged to the lobby of the church and got ready to greet the saints. Now of course, I did not want to do it. I was mad, and I did not want to smile and shake hands. As the congregation departed, God used them to break my heart and shut my mouth. It was a lesson in humility that changed my life. The first man who greeted me pressed a check into my hand. In my cynicism I slipped it into my pocket, believing that it was the gas honorarium. But another man followed him and opened my coat pocket. He sweetly stuffed some cash in it, shook my hand, and walked away. Before I knew what was happening, my clothing became an offering plate. Money was falling out on the floor as people continued to use my coat as a receptacle. One twenty-dollar bill fell in front of me on the floor. I quickly kicked it behind me! Not because of selfishness but because of embarrassment!

Not one word had been publicly stated concerning a love offering. There had been no plea given, and no plates were passed. Yet, when I got back to my room and counted the money, I began to weep. Those precious people had given over $1,200! All of it had been stuffed in my shirt and coat pockets! As tears raced down my face, I fell down beside the bed. On my knees, I begged my Father to forgive my faithlessness. I praised Him for His grace and patience in my life. I promised Him that I would continue to trust Him to meet my needs. And

I made a fresh commitment to continue to honor Him with tithes and offerings. Since that landmark day, many things have changed about the evangelism ministry that God has called me into. But one thing remains constant – My God is faithful and true!

He has miraculously, consistently, gloriously opened the windows of heaven, and poured out His blessings. Luke 6:38 says, *Give, and it shall be given unto you; good measure, pressed down, and shaken together, and running over, shall men give into your bosom. For with the same measure that ye mete* [measure] *withal it shall be measured to you again.*

About ten years ago our ministry claimed this verse and decided to stand upon it. We have supported Bible college students, missionaries, evangelists, and churches around the world. Now, that is not a boast, it is a blessing! Every single time someone new is added to the mission list, I get excited. It just means that God is about to bless us in a fresh new way! God has a supernatural cycle of sufficiency that just keeps on flowing. And the best way to get under the spout is to honor God with your tithe. Then, really watch it pour out as you go beyond that and love God by giving an offering. Give something special to help your church. Buy your pastor a new suit, or give him money to take his wife to dinner! Support some ministry or missionary. Open your eyes and become aware of what God is doing in different parts of the world. It is really true that you cannot out-give God!

* * * *

It is always a wonderful thing to see a believer get excited about giving. Since 1990 our ministry has had summer student camps in the mountains of Tennessee. The camp is called PowerLife, and God has abundantly blessed it. That first year we had a total enrollment of 125. Now, over 1200 students per year attend PowerLife! Of course it takes a hard working staff to administrate and minister these camps. Some of the most dedicated and diligent staffers are volunteers. Pastor Doyce Thompson and his wife Mildred are good examples of that. I met Brother Doyce when I preached a revival at his church in Bogalusa, Louisiana. After his retirement in the mid 1990s, Doyce and Mildred returned to their home state of Tennessee. Since our camp was at a college campus near them, this precious couple began to assist us during PowerLife. They would help set up tables, or carry equipment, or even shuttle our guests to the airport and back.

Why, Sister Mildred would even keep a nursery for the small children of our leaders! There was no task too small or no job too menial for these selfless servants of God. And during those years, I was under the mistaken impression that the host college was paying them something to help us. After all, Brother Doyce was a big help to them, too. And from all indications, I thought he was receiving some small remuneration from the college conference office. But one day I discovered that no pay had ever been given the Thompsons. The Spirit of God burdened my heart to bless these dear people who had done so much to help us.

One night during one of the camp worship services, I spoke to the students about the need. It was the last week of camp and there were about six hundred students there. The Thompsons were not in the service that night. (They were keeping the nursery.) I told the students how much Doyce and Mildred had done for PowerLife. I reminded them that most of the time they were behind the scenes, but they were always working hard to keep the camp running. Then I explained to them that they had never been paid, and it was time. Now, bear in mind that these six hundred students were all middle and high school students (grades 6-12). Basically, the only extra money that they had was snack bar money. But I shared with them that God wanted to use them to bless the Thompsons. I also told them that God always opens heaven and pours blessings out on those who sacrificially give. Someone spoke up and said, "Let's give right now!" Our staff grabbed small boxes, containers, and anything else they could find. As these temporary offering plates were passed, our worship leader led in praise and singing. The money was counted and the service continued.

That night twenty-six students were saved, and another twenty were called into vocational ministry. Some student leaders who were discouraged received a touch from the Lord and publicly testified about it. Others experienced great spiritual renewal and victory. What I am trying to say is this: The glory of God fell! There was a freedom and a fire that fell on the camp that night. Then after all of that, we called the Thompsons from the nursery to the platform. As I presented them with the offering, those students suddenly stood and shouted with joy. I want you to know that those six hundred students had offered their snack money and extra spending money. When all of the coins and bills were counted, the love offering to Doyce and Mildred was over $1,600! Everyone who was there was blessed beyond measure.

But that is not the end of the story. The one thing that I will never forget is what happened at lunch the next day. I was standing in the cafeteria when a seventh-grade boy walked up to me and handed me two dollars. He said, "Brother Rick, this is for the offering. I left my wallet in my room last night, and I wanted to give this to the Thompsons."

I looked at the small bills and then I said something stupid. I replied, "Son, they received a wonderful offering last night. Why don't you keep this, you may need it later this week."

That thirteen-year-old boy innocently looked at me and said, "But God told me to give that. I don't want to miss a blessing!"

It so overwhelmed me that I instantly embraced that young man. I asked for his forgiveness, and I told him that I would deliver his gift to Brother Doyce. As he turned to walk away, that young man raised a clenched fist and punched the air. Then he loudly spoke to no one in particular and said, "Yes! Look out blessing, here I come!"

Several months later I was in a revival meeting at a church outside of Birmingham, Alabama. I was preaching one night about giving, and I told that whole camp experience to the congregation. Then it suddenly hit me, and I said, "Wouldn't it be wonderful if our churches got as excited about giving as that thirteen-year-old boy! Picture the offering plates being passed on Sunday. As they get near the back, some impatient man leaps to his feet and screams, Hurry up and get those plates back here! I can't wait to get a blessing!" Of course you realize that I made that statement kind of "tongue in cheek." It sounded good to say and the audience responded with laughter. But the next night at that very revival, that actual thing happened. The plates were being solemnly passed. The church organist was slowly playing what sounded like a funeral march. In the quiet dignity of that moment, a deep, resonant voice pierced the air. Out of a gathering of about three hundred, one man shouted, "Hurry up with those plates! I need a blessing!"

The crowd let out a collective gasp and then suddenly broke out into unrestrained laughing and clapping. From the front pew I instantly turned around and saw what everyone was cheering about. Standing about three rows from the back was the man who had joyously interrupted the service. He was grinning and waving some money in his hand. I found out later that he was one of the quietest men in the church. The pastor told me that he would consider that man the most unlikely to do what he did. He stood there smiling until the plate came his way and he gave.

As he sat down, people were once again applauding. It was a moment of sheer unrehearsed, unplanned, impromptu excitement. That man had understood the joy of giving. And I was certainly thrilled by it. After all, it was my love offering that they were taking up!

In 2 Corinthians 9:7 the Scripture declares, *For God loveth a cheerful giver.* It is an exciting thing to see someone who has been liberated when it comes to giving. The Bible gives us a compelling example in the book of

Exodus. Moses was commanded to build the tabernacle. He gathered the children of Israel together and received an offering to raise money. The people were challenged to give willingly for the work of the Lord. In Exodus chapters 35 and 36, an amazing thing happened. God's man had to ask the people to stop giving! *Let neither man nor woman make any more work for the offering of the sanctuary. So the people were restrained from bringing. For the stuff they had was sufficient for all the work to make it, and too much* (Exodus 36:6-7).

Wouldn't it be wonderful for a modern day pastor to stand and say, "You people need to quit giving so much. We have more than enough!" That could actually happen if all the members of our churches became tithers instead of tippers.

Chapter 8

Forty-eight Dollars

When I stop to think about it, I am greatly ashamed that I have ever doubted my God's faithfulness to provide for me in evangelism. After all, it was through a love offering that God called me to be an evangelist. I was a thirty-four-year-old pastor in Fernandina Beach, Florida, when it happened.

One day I was opening my mail when I saw a brochure advertising a new evangelism conference. It was a Real Evangelism Conference sponsored by Bailey Smith. The conference was to feature some of my real heroes in the faith. Along with Dr. Smith would be Evangelists Junior Hill and Bill Stafford. Dr. Jerry Vines, as well as other great men of God, would also be preaching. I knew that I needed a personal revival, and this conference would help supply just that. Within a matter of minutes my secretary had made plane and hotel reservations for my Student Minister and me to attend the Marietta, Georgia, conference. I had no idea that my life and ministry was about to be radically changed.

It was on a Thursday evening in February at the Real Evangelism Conference. I sat high in the balcony at the Roswell Street Baptist Church. An appeal was made for the love offering. Now, there was no fee to attend the conference, but a love offering was being taken to help defray the great expense of the conference. The Holy Spirit put His hand on my wallet, and I immediately had the impression that I was to give the entire contents. Well, I pulled out my wallet and checked on what I had. There wasn't a great deal there, but there were two twenties, a five, and three one-dollar bills. That meant a grand total of forty-eight dollars. I began to calculate how much money I would need to get through the next twenty-four hours of the conference. There was dinner that night and two meals the next day. (Breakfast was provided at the hotel.) Of course my flight home had been paid, but I knew that I needed to eat. So, I carried on a rather intense private conversation with God.

As the offering buckets got closer, I had this over-whelming burden to give all forty-eight dollars. Yet, I knew that if I did that, there would be nothing left. There were no credit cards with me, and I knew that God did not want me to go to the ATM. He was asking me to give everything and then to trust Him. At the same time, there was this incredible feeling that God was going to speak to me in a life changing way! However, I was still in this spiritual tug of war about what to do. I proposed to God that maybe I should give only half of it. In my heart I knew it was all or nothing, but I continued bargaining with the Father. Before I knew it, the offering bucket was in front of me. Quietly and quickly, I pulled out all my cash and dropped it in. Then I did something rather strange. I watched that bucket as it went all the way down the aisle. For one fleeting instance, I had the greatest urge to go after it!

Minutes later, still a bit uneasy, I listened to Dr. Jerry Vines preach on soul winning. During the altar call, God broke my heart. I knelt in the aisle and asked the Lord to renew my passion to see lost people changed. I didn't realize it at that moment, but that is when God gave me the burden to become an evangelist. I had forgotten all about that forty-eight bucks until my student minister reminded me that it was time to eat. I started to ask him to loan me some money, but I didn't think I was supposed to. I said, "All right Father, I am going to trust you."

So, we went out to eat with several other preacher friends. They all ordered big dinners. I was hungry too, but I had more pride than faith. Finally, I just ordered a small dessert and figured I could bum the money from someone later. As we finished eating, something incredible took place. One of the pastors at the table was a dear friend of mine. I had recently had the privilege of preaching a revival in his church. As we stood up to leave, he reached over for my bill. He said, "Oh Brother, I meant to tell you earlier, I want to pay your check. I wish you had ordered more." He grabbed it up and walked away. I watched him as he headed for the cashier, and I thought, "What a dummy; I could have had steak!"

The next day I was walking out of church after the morning session. Suddenly, I felt someone take me by the arm. I turned and recognized a pastor friend from my home state of Florida. He smiled and said these words, "Brother Rick, I have been looking for you! God told me to take you to lunch!" Well, by now I was ready to trust the Lord! This was one of the most exciting experiences of my life.

When it came time for dinner that evening, I was walking in faith. I could hardly wait to get to the restaurant to see who would buy my meal! Sure enough, another brother stepped up and said, "My treat." God had met my every need. I left that conference with a greater passion to reach the lost. I left there with a wonderful lesson of faith. And a few weeks later, I realized that I had received God's wonderful call to be a full-time vocational evangelist. I didn't think anymore about that forty-eight dollars – for about two days.

On that Monday I was sitting at my desk when my secretary brought in the mail. There was a letter from Mike and Karen. I had preached their wedding the year before. When Mike tried to pay me, I refused. I knew they were struggling financially. Also, they were among the most faithful, spiritual young adults in our church. It was a real delight to be part of their wedding. So, I told them to keep the money and use it on their honeymoon. Shortly after that, Mike got a great promotion. They had moved to another state, and our church sorely missed them. As I opened the letter, I was anxious to read about how they were doing. The envelope contained a check that was written to me. The letter from Mike explained how God had burdened his heart to send me something. I looked down at the check and saw two things – the amount was for fifty dollars, and the date on the check was that Thursday when God burdened me to give Him all that was in my wallet! I quietly rose from the desk and gently closed the door. Then I had myself a shouting spell!

God had changed my life and future through that Real Evangelism Conference. Little did I realize how much. Eight years later, He gave me the privilege to preach at a Real Evangelism Conference! There are no words to describe how it felt to be invited to preach at the place that redirected my ministry. Since then, God has allowed me to preach in many more conferences. Dr. Bailey Smith has been such a mentor and friend. God has used him as a great instrument of influence in my life. So many blessings have come my way since that glorious February night many years ago.

But before I close this chapter, let me tell you about one blessing in particular. In the late 1990s, I was invited to speak at Real Evangelism. In one of the morning sessions, I was scheduled to preach with two other men. Those two men happened to be two of my heroes. I am talking about Dr. Junior Hill and Dr. Bill Stafford. These men are two of the greatest evangelists in the history of Southern Baptists. When I was a young pastor, I would drive great distances to hear them. If I heard of a conference where they were speaking, I made arrangements to be there. I do not believe I would have gone to that fateful February conference had they not been there. Now, God had given a puny preacher like me the honor of preaching with them! So, on that wonderful morning, I just sat there and cried. I thought about that evening in the balcony that seemed so long ago. I thought about that forty-eight dollars that God convicted me about. I also thought of how a faithless young pastor tried to hold on to it. And I just sat there and praised God for His goodness.

In the last chapter we discussed the first part of Malachi 3:10. The latter part of that verse is the most exciting. God Himself promises, *Prove me now herewith, saith the Lord of hosts, if I will not open you the windows of heaven, and pour you out a **blessing**, that there shall not be room enough to receive it.* I love the familiar story of the old farmer. He would harvest his crop and then give most of it away. He would help the hungry and hurting people of his community. Yet, he still always seemed to have an abundance left for him and his family. One day a fellow asked, "I don't understand. How can you keep giving so much away and still you seem to never run out?"

The old farmer smiled and replied, "It's simple. You see, I believe in the shovel principle."

The confused man looked at the farmer and questioned, "What is the shovel principle?"

The farmer wisely answered, "Well, it works like this. I keep shoveling into God's bin, and God keeps shoveling into my bin. And remember, God has a bigger shovel!" Remember that it really is *More blessed to give than to receive* (Acts 20:35). Whether it is forty-eight cents, forty-eight dollars, or forty-eight thousand dollars, be sure to remember that God already owns it all! We should always be willing to give all that He asks us to give.

Chapter 9

It's What's Inside That Counts

People who do not live in Florida do not understand how cold North Florida can get in the winter. Obviously, it does not stay cold very long, but it is still cold. It is a different kind of cold air. The climate produces a wet chill that can cut right through you. When we do get one of those damp, dreary days, I like to use the fireplace. One cold winter afternoon I decided to light a fire. I keep the firewood stacked up against the wooden fence in the backyard. Well, I was rummaging through it and picking out the driest, best wood to burn. My wheelbarrow was almost full when I reached for one more log to put in. It was a good, firm, dry piece of oak, but as I picked it up, the wood literally fell apart in my hands. That pretty piece of wood was absolutely decayed and full of bugs. There was a whole community of roaches living inside that log. I am talking about those big black Florida roaches – the ones that look like they are on steroids! Well, I quickly dropped what was left of that wood. I couldn't believe it was that rotten. After all, it looked just as whole as the other wood I had already loaded. The outside showed no deterioration at all. Amazingly, despite how good the outside looked, the inside was ugly, wasted, and useless. I was fooled by it because I could only see the outside.

The same thing is true when we look at other people. We can only look on the outside of a person. However, our great Creator knows the real story, because God looks inside. You see, there are people who wear designer clothes and still have a dirty character.

Some folks have a pretty face and still have an ugly heart. All around us are individuals who are all made up on the outside and all messed up on the inside. And yet, it is a sobering thing to realize that God knows all about all of us. First Samuel 16:7 says, *For the Lord seeth not as man seeth; for man looketh on the outward appearance, but the Lord looketh on the heart.* That means that God knows the *real* me. Because of that, I have purposed in my heart to quit spending all my time looking at everyone else. I have decided to try to spend more time examining myself because there are times in which I am the one who is rotten.

One year at our PowerLife Student Camp, I came to that realization in a rather humorous way. Every summer we have a big shaving cream war on the last day of camp. It really is sort of controlled chaos. Teenagers will be teenagers, and that means that some come to camp with pranks on their minds. As an incentive to hold down the practical jokes, we promise them a big shaving cream war. The rule is simple – If they keep the cream in the cans during the week, they can release it all on

Friday. The whole thing really is a Kodak moment and a video memory. We put all of the leaders in the center of the field. Hundreds of students form a huge ring around them. Everyone is armed with a can or two of shaving cream. Our recreation minister blows a whistle and, well, you get the picture!

For the first seven or eight years of PowerLife, I was involved in the war. I don't do it anymore because I am the leader of the camp, and I don't have to if I don't want to! Besides that, I got my fill of shaving cream those first few years. It gets in your ears, and your eyes, and your mouth. The stuff burns, and stings, and tastes awful! And those are the reasons that led us to a regrettable and dubious decision.

One year one of our brilliant leaders suggested that we use whipping cream instead of shaving cream. It all sounded logical and reasonable. The whipping cream would not burn, and it would be more pleasant to swallow. And so, we advertised to all our church groups to bring whipping cream to camp. The day of the big war arrived. We gathered in the field of battle with our weapons of whipping cream. Yes, I was in the war that year, but I believe that it was my last war. You see, none of us rocket scientists had considered the fact that the cream had not been refrigerated. When it was emptied into our eager hands, it was exposed to the summer sun.

There are not enough adjectives that I could use to describe the odor. The mere words *reek, stench, putrid, stagnant*, and *nauseating* do not accurately describe the smell. Now, we did smell it during the battle. It was after the war had ended that we were made aware of the wounded.

I got hosed off, trudged up to my dorm room, and took a shower. Then, I sat down in a chair and looked over my drama script for the concluding service that night. Quickly I became alert to the fact that there was a horrible aroma. My wife Judy was in the room. I looked at her and said, "Do you smell that?"

She quizzically answered back, "Smell what?"

I was stunned that she could not smell that nasty odor. So I dramatically replied, "That sour, rotten smell. It stinks in this room!" I made the mistake of suggesting that perhaps there were dirty clothes she had not cleaned. The look on her face made me realize that I needed to change the subject. I instantly stood to my feet and declared, "I have got to get out of this room."

Well, I walked out into the hallway, and the smell was still there. I said, "Whew, it stinks out here in the hall. Something must be in this carpet!" Immediately I became critical of the housekeepers. All I knew was that I had to get away from that terrible, suffocating fragrance. Finally, I walked outside and came to the same sad conclusion. Taking a whiff, I announced, "It stinks out here!" Since I needed to blame it on somebody, I criticized the maintenance staff. I thought that perhaps they were having a sewer problem of some sort. All I knew was this one thing – There is something on this campus that stinks.

An hour or so later, it was time for dinner. I got my serving tray, picked up my food, and sat down to eat. When I leaned over my plate to get a bite, I swiftly put down my fork. As incredible as it seemed, I announced,

"My food stinks!" About that moment one of our staff leaders sat down beside me. I looked over at him, twitched my nose, and said, "Brother, I love you, but you stink!"

He looked back at me and returned the compliment when he said, "So do you!" It was in that moment of revelation that it hit me right in the nose. It wasn't the clothes, or the carpet, or the sewer, or the food that stunk. It was me! In fact, it was all of us! Here is what happened: Although we had showered and cleaned up, that sour whipping cream had lined the inside of our nostrils. That sour smell was inside each of us. There is no way that I can express to you how it smelled when we all gathered in the auditorium that night.

But as bad as the smell was, we all learned a lesson. Well, actually we learned two lessons. The first lesson was this – no more whipping cream. The second lesson was by far the most valuable one of all. It was the lesson that reminded us (especially me) that before you criticize others, you had better examine yourself, because occasionally there is something *inside* that needs to be cleaned out. The first step to revival is found in Psalm 139:23. That powerful verse declares, *Search me, O God, and know my heart.* That is an invitation to the Holy Spirit to walk down every hall of our heart. It is a request for Him to open every closet and pull back every curtain. True spiritual restoration, renewal, and revival begin with a heart exam. However, we must be willing to let the Great Physician do the examination. Remember, He is the only one who sees us just as we are.

* * * *

It is a terrible thing to get sick when you are away from home. Thankfully, there have only been a few times when that has happened to me. One of those times occurred in the state of South Carolina. The revival had just started on Sunday, but by Monday morning I was very ill. A sinus infection had wrapped around my vocal cords and taken my voice. The small town that I was in did not have a doctor that could see me quickly. There was no way that I could wait two days for an appointment. So I went down to the small county hospital. It was a quaint little one-story hospital, but it did have an emergency room. Now, emergency rooms can be depressing, but you would think a Monday morning in a small town would be quiet. But on this particular Monday it had all broken loose. That tiny little room was filled with emergencies.

I checked in at the desk and sat down to wait. As I looked around me, I saw and heard some awful things. Sitting in front of me was a construction worker who had been injured on the job. He had somehow cut his right arm. The poor guy was holding his arm, but blood was slowly seeping through. I felt sorry for him, and I wanted the busy nurses to hurry up and take him back to a room.

To my left was a young girl who had been injured at her school. She appeared to be about twelve or thirteen years old. The young lady was wearing gym clothes. Her right eye was very badly swollen. It was obvious she had been hit by a ball of some sort. The mother of the girl was trying to comfort her by holding a wet cloth against her throbbing head. I hate to see children hurting, and I was praying silently for her.

On my right was a woman in apparent agony. This

dear lady appeared to have some type of stomach ailment. She was bent over and holding her midsection. The aching woman was softly moaning as she slowly rocked back and forth. My heart went out to her, and I was hoping that she would soon be able to see the doctor.

Finally, sitting right by me, there was a small child who looked to be two or three years old. This little girl had some kind of virus or flu bug. You could tell by looking into her eyes that she had a high fever. Suddenly, the child lurched forward and vomited on the floor. Her frantic mother was screaming, the child was crying, and I was starting to get nauseous.

I surveyed everything that was going on around me. Not only did everyone in that room look sick, but they all sounded sick as well. All I could hear was crying, moaning, and hurting noises. It was like stereo coming from every side. Sick "surround sound" was playing, and the volume was turned up!

At that very moment I decided to get up and go back to the hotel. I mean, these people needed a doctor worse than I did. I really did not want a doc wasting his time on me when there were so many others who were in more critical condition than I was. After all, I could just go back to my room and gargle some warm salt water.

So I arose from my seat to leave that emergency room. On the way out, I thought it would be courteous to tell the receptionist that I was leaving. As I passed by the water cooler, I stopped to get a drink. I could hardly swallow that small sip of water. My throat was inflamed, and I realized that I had some type of infection. Very quietly I slipped back to my seat and waited my turn to see the doctor.

Now, I want you to think about that for a moment. Even though my illness was not as visible as everyone else in that waiting room, I still needed medical attention. The other patients who were sitting in that emergency room had obvious infirmities. I could look at each of them and tell what was wrong. One needed stitches, another had a head injury, and one had a painful stomach disorder. Even the small child could not hide her sickness, but not one of those patients could look at me and tell what my sickness was.

In fact, no one could tell by looking at me from the outside. Only the educated, well-trained eye of a doctor could diagnose my malady and prescribe the proper cure. And even then, the doctor would have to look at me on the inside. Only then could he accurately suggest what medicine I would need to take away the infection.

There is some spiritual sickness that is easy to spot. On some people the disease is obvious. They are so infected by the world that the scars of sin cannot be hidden. But there are others who hide their illness very well. They have successfully hidden their sin sickness from their family and their friends. Some are even adept at fooling their pastors, their Bible classes, and even their churches.

But there is one Person who cannot ever be fooled. His name is Doctor Jesus, and He knows all about me from the inside to the outside. His penetrating light always examines me and exposes me. *Neither is there any creature that is not manifest in His sight: but all things are naked and opened unto the eyes of Him with whom we have to do* (Hebrews 4:13*)*.

There are times in the Christian life when we get unhealthy spiritually. Those are the times that we need a personal examination from the Great Physician. Sometimes He will adjust our spiritual diet or prescribe just the healing medicine that we need. But there are those times that spiritual surgery is required and something has to be removed. Whatever the case, He always knows precisely what we need because He knows what is on the inside of each of us. It is our inside that God is the most concerned about. After all, it is what's inside that counts!

Chapter 10

When the Horn Gets Stuck

I drive a lot of rental cars. Some of my revival meetings are held in churches that are located far away from major airports. Often it is easier on the pastor and the church for me just to rent a car. That way no one has to drive a great distance to get me or return me to the airport. Also, it provides transportation for me during the week.

Now, I have rented cars from every major company. Most of them are reputable and reliable. They try their best to maintain and take care of their vehicles. However, I believe that their job is almost impossible. In order to make money, the vehicles need to constantly stay on the road. Many times they are not properly serviced. Also, rental cars are abused by the people who rent them. Because of that, there are times you can get a car that may look good, but it is not in the best mechanical condition. And then there are those times when you rent a car that is in bad shape, but it is not the engine that stinks. There is nothing worse than getting a car that has just been turned in by a chain smoker – whoa! But fortunately, I have not had that many rental car inconveniences. However, there was one time that was unforgettable. Not only will I never forget it, but neither will anyone else who was within earshot. It was the day when the horn got stuck.

It happened after a revival meeting in Anniston, Alabama. Anniston is located about two hours from the Atlanta airport. When I preach in that area of Alabama, I usually fly to Atlanta, rent a car, and drive. That is easier than waiting in Atlanta to change planes and then shuttle to the closest airport, which would be Birmingham.

So I drove from Atlanta to Anniston to preach what turned out to be an absolutely glorious revival. The church was refreshing, the crowds were big, and the worship services were exciting. And, not only did the church experience true revival, but there was also a great evangelistic harvest of souls. It was just a good, old-fashioned, camp meeting type of revival!

After the last service ended, the pastor gave me my love offering check. I was overwhelmed with the amount of money that sweet church had given me. On the way back to my hotel, I wept and thanked God for His goodness. I thought about the wonderful way in which my Father was blessing my ministry. In fact, the Anniston revival was just the latest in a string of four or five fantastic revival meetings! It was in that attitude of gratitude that I happily packed my clothes for the trip home.

I checked my airline ticket and was reminded that I had an early flight out of Atlanta. The flight was scheduled for nine o'clock in the morning. I began to calculate my time schedule. I knew it would take two hours to drive, plus

I needed to allow an extra thirty minutes to turn in the car. Since I wanted to be at the airport by eight o'clock, I decided to leave at 5:30 a.m. That meant that I had to get up at about five o'clock. Just before I set my wake-up call, a mildly disturbing fact hit me. Since Anniston was in the Central time zone, I was going to lose an hour driving back to Atlanta. I briefly scolded myself for getting such an early flight back. I think I referred to myself as "dummy" because I did not account for that hour when I booked the ticket. Oh well, I was so utterly happy, I determined that nothing was going to steal my joy. So, I set the wake-up call for 4:00 a.m. and went to bed.

It seemed that I had just gotten to sleep when that irritating phone blasted me out of slumber. As I got up to get dressed, I was still thinking about the revival. Once again, I found myself praising God for the abundant way He was pouring Himself on my life, my family, and my ministry! When I headed down Interstate 20, I was wired up and wide awake. I could not remember a time when I felt so good about everything. Our family was healthy and happy. The ministry was exciting and experiencing a season of financial freedom. I thought about how far ahead my calendar was booked, and I praised God for it. Then I began to think how fulfilling it was to be doing exactly what God had planned for my life.

Suddenly, I became so overwhelmed with joy that I began to sing! Now, I am one terrible singer. Thankfully, no one else was in the car! God is certainly aware that I am never going to be a music evangelist. But He is not interested in our harmony; He is interested in our hearts. And that morning my heart was extremely full as I praised and worshipped my wonderful Lord. I was thanking Him for everything. I thanked Him for the beautiful sun that was coming up. I thanked Him for the scenery that was around me. Why, I even thanked Him for Delta Airlines that was taking me home.

One hour passed swiftly, and I quickly found myself in the busy outer traffic of Atlanta. Traffic can really be a source of frustration and stress for me. But not on this glad day! I was convinced that my joy could not be stolen by a little bitty traffic jam. It was about that time that I left I-20 and exited on the Camp Creek highway. That is the highly congested road that leads to the airport. On this particular Thursday morning, it was bumper-to-bumper traffic that was moving at about 60 miles per hour.

Even though I was surrounded by a multitude of rush hour commuters, I was still having my private little worship service. It was just me and Jesus in that little Chevrolet. That is when it happened. I was in the left hand lane when a car on the right tried to move over. Obviously, I was in the other driver's blind spot, and he never saw me. So I blew the horn to let him know that I was there. He quickly moved back over, and an accident was averted. As I hurriedly moved past him, he smiled and waved at me. I could read his lips as he mouthed the words, "I'm sorry." I waved back and smiled. It was an honest mistake that every driver has made at one time or the other.

But there was just one minor problem. The horn that I had pressed was still blowing. Somehow it had gotten stuck. So, I calmly mashed it again. Well, it continued to blow. I began to hit it with a little bit more aggression, but it would not quit blowing! Then I started beating on it! That ear-splitting horn seemed to get louder and louder! Of course by now my worship service had come to an end. To say the least, I was getting slightly overwrought.

I was still about forty-five minutes from the airport. I was not on the interstate anymore. The road that I was traveling on was a very busy thoroughfare that had traffic lights on it. Here I am with a horn blowing and it won't quit. Well, I came to a red light, and I had to stop. It gave me a chance to look for a fuse box. Sadly, I could not find one. The horn was still blowing, and there appeared to be nothing that I could do to stop it. Slowly I turned my head and looked around me at the other drivers who were waiting at the light. Most of them were angrily staring at me. Two or three gave me a hand gesture. I knew that they were not signaling to me that I was number one!

The light turned green, but I was still red. About that time I saw a sign that said, "Mechanic On Duty." I pulled off the road and quickly sped to his garage. A man wearing overalls and carrying a wrench walked out. He screamed, "Hey, your horn is blowing." I assured him that I already knew that. Then he lifted the hood and looked inside. After a minute or so he closed the hood and said, "These new cars are so tight under there that you can't reach anything, I'm sorry, I can't help you." As I pulled out of his garage, my horn was still blaring. I was stunned that a mechanic could not stop a blowing horn. At any rate, I was getting a little short on time. So I had to keep moving.

This great morning had turned into a nightmare! For about thirty more minutes, I drove on with that horn blowing. People were staring at me, and some were still saluting me in their own unique way. By now I was really upset. I was frantically trying to weave through traffic and return that piece of junk car! My stomach was churning, and my hands were sweating.

It was at that moment that I realized that I needed to get gas. I was supposed to return that car with a full tank. Spotting a gas station, I pulled up to the pump and tried to look inconspicuous. As I was pumping the gas, a woman walked out to get in her car. She stopped, stood there, and stared at me. I nervously glanced back at her. Finally, she spoke, "Sir, did you know that your horn is blowing?"

There were many things I wanted to say to that woman. But I am thankful that I was able to compose myself long enough to quietly say, "Yes, ma'am, I know it. The horn is stuck and I can't fix it."

Embarrassed and exasperated, I got back in the loud car and continued my journey. When I saw the car rental parking lot, I nearly screamed in relief. I parked that lousy car and got my luggage out in record time. One of the employees walked over and started to speak. I tersely interrupted him and said, "I know, the horn is blowing. But I can't stop it." I settled my account with him and almost ran to get on the shuttle to go to the airport.

Once on board that bus, I literally collapsed down into that seat. As we were leaving, I turned back and saw an amazing sight. There were four men surrounding that car! The hood was open, and all four of them were staring underneath it. All the while that horn was still blowing!

A passenger on the bus looked over at me. He laughed as he said, "I don't think they can stop it from blowing."

I gazed back at the car one last time. Then I facetiously said, "I know how to stop it. Put a stick of dynamite under it."

Later, I was comfortably seated on that jet as I winged my way homeward. The noise in my ears had finally stopped ringing. My blood pressure had returned to normal, and my stomach had finally settled down. Then I thought about what had transpired in just a few hours. As I reflected, I thought, "Didn't I begin this morning singing? Wasn't I praising God earlier today?" I mused as I thought of how quickly a sweet morning had turned sour. A day that had started out so good had gone badly so fast. I had left my hotel feeling on top of the world. But before the morning was over, I felt like jumping off the world. Isn't it interesting how swiftly our emotions can change?

Then I thought about the great prophet of God named Elijah when he boldly stood before wicked King Ahab in 1 Kings 18:21 and declared, *How long halt ye between two opinions? If the Lord be God, follow Him: but if Baal, then follow him.* Then the Bible declares how he challenged hundreds of false prophets to a contest. Elijah told them to call on their gods, and he would call on his God. He proposed that the first God that answered with fire would be the only God!

What an incredible challenge. There has never been an athletic competition that equals it. The winner would be called the one and only, true and living God.

It was the Omnipotent Olympics. You could call it the Supernatural Bowl.

And 1 Kings 18 dramatically describes how Jehovah God used Elijah as His instrument to call down fire! It is one of the greatest examples of boldness and confidence in all of history. One man dared to stand against wickedness and idolatry. One man dared to believe God. One man dared to publicly stand and announce that His God would come through.

But just a few verses later, that one man is a picture of utter despair, discouragement, and defeat. In 1 Kings 19 one demonic woman announces that she is going to kill him, and God's great warrior becomes a wimp and runs. Then this mighty champion makes a stunning request. *It is enough; now O Lord, take away my life; for I am not better than my fathers* (1 Kings 19:4). In a short span of time, Elijah went from the penthouse to the poorhouse. He slipped from the mountain of victory and fell headfirst into the valley of defeat.

We can learn much from the great men and women of the Bible. Here is a valuable lesson taught to us through the life of Elijah. It reminds us that joy can be stolen in a moment. Do you know how far it is from Hallelujah Highway to Sorrow Street? The distance is not very far at all. You can get there quickly. The circumstances of life can whisk you from Amen Avenue to Bad News Boulevard in the blink of an eye.

What do you do when your day suddenly turns bad? What happens to you when the horn gets stuck? It is easy to focus on our circumstances. When we don't have an explanation, we sometimes sink into exasperation. But we don't live by explanations; we live by the promises of God. The devil wants us to look at the problem, but God wants us to live by the promises. As we travel life's highway, our horn will occasionally get stuck. Don't let the noise take the song out of your heart!

Chapter 11

Amen!

It is exciting to be in church when God gets in the house! Now, I know that God does not live in a church building. We are the temple that God lives in. That is why corporate worship is so vital for all believers. When the family of God gets together in one place, well, all heaven breaks loose! In fact, our worship services really ought to be "heaven on earth."

I am sorry to report that is not the case in some congregations. There really are many dull, dry, dead churches in America. I heard about the old country preacher who was preaching a revival in a dead, dry church. He said, "This church is as dry as cracker juice!" Brother, let me tell you that is dry!

What do you think is the definition of a church that is alive? There are all kinds of interpretations. Some people think a church is dead if there is not a constant clamor of shouting, clapping, and noise. Well, that is just not true. In the Old Testament when the glory of God fell, people were on their faces in holy reverence. Just because you are noisy does not necessarily mean you are spiritual. I have preached in some churches where they try to outshout the preacher. It is exhausting to be in a place like that. But I need to point out that I do like some verbal affirmation when I preach. I love to hear people say, "Amen!"

Over these years I have met some memorable people in the churches I have visited. I have heard some unusual responses come from the direction of the pews. I have had the wonderful privilege to preach to thousands of folks. And yet, in all of those thousands, there are four men who stand out in my mind. They stand out not only because of the unusual things they shouted while I was preaching, but they stand out because each of those four men deeply loves Jesus. Not one of them was ever trying to be heard or call any individual attention to themselves.

The first one lives in the big state of Texas. He is a deacon in his church, and he is a fervent witness. His name is Scott and he has a pretty large business, but he is unapologetically unashamed of Christ. I was preaching in his church one night, and suddenly I heard Brother Scott say, "That's what the Bible says!" I love that.

The second man is from Bristol, Tennessee. He is a dear brother named Phil Whitaker. As a matter of fact, he is the worship leader at his church. I go to that wonderful church every summer, and Brother Phil has done the same thing for years. Right before I get up to preach, he will walk over and grab my hand. He looks me in the eye and shouts, "Preach, preach, preach!" Son, that fires me up!

The next brother is from a large church in Alabama.

His name is Ed. While I was there, Brother Ed hollered out, "You said a mouthful!" Now, Brother Ed is proud to be a redneck, but he is happier about the fact that he is redeemed.

Then there are two men from Florida. Both of them live in Jacksonville. One of them is Brother Don. The first time I preached a revival at his church, I heard this loud, piercing voice. Brother Don said, "You're on it now!" The other Florida man is a brother I had the privilege to pastor. His name is Bill Crane. I was Brother Bill's pastor when God called me into evangelism. Once, I was at a revival in Jacksonville, and I didn't know Brother Bill was visiting that night. Then I heard this familiar voice declare, "Think about it!" I knew Brother Bill was there.

Once I thought that it would be wonderful to be preaching and have those five men together in one service. Then it occurred to me that they might get me so pumped up that I would preach myself to death! If I died before the rapture, that would surely be the way to go!

But then I came up with another idea. Wouldn't it be good to get all of them shouting on one tape recording? Then I could just carry it with me and give the tape to the sound technician. If I were preaching in a dead church, I could give the technician a signal. All of a sudden the congregation would hear these words:

"That's what the Bible says!"

"You've said a mouthful!"

"You're on it now!"

"Think about it!"

"Preach, preach, preach!"

Actually, giving verbal affirmation to the preacher

is biblical. In the book of Nehemiah we have a record of one of the greatest revival meetings in history. God used Nehemiah to rebuild the broken-down wall around the city of Jerusalem. After the wall was restored, it was time for revival. Evangelist Ezra came to town to do the preaching. Nehemiah 8:5-6 says, *And Ezra opened the book in the sight of all the people; (for he was above all the people;) and when he had opened it, all the people stood up: And Ezra blessed the Lord, the great God. And all the people answered,* **Amen, Amen,** *with lifting up their hands; and they bowed their heads, and worshipped the Lord with faces to the ground.*

The word *amen* means "to tell the truth." It is a word of acknowledgement and encouragement. There are times when you can audibly mention that word in a worship service. Don't say it just so you are heard; say it to encourage your pastor. Shout it to voice your confidence in the truth of God's Holy Word. Speak it to announce to the demons of hell that you believe the Book! Amen!

Chapter 12

Somebody is in My Room

During the course of a year, I will stay in hotel rooms between 175 to 200 days. I have stayed in just about every kind of hotel room that exists. Some are elegant and expensive, while others are cheap and cheesy. I have stayed in some suites that are so beautiful they will take your breath away. But I have also stayed in some dumps so awful they will take your breath away! However, I can honestly say that over these years there have only been a handful of bad experiences.

My hotel room is literally my home away from home. All of us have our little idiosyncrasies. I suppose that is just a nice way of saying that all of us are a little weird. Anyway, I have some weird traits when it comes to my hotel room. For instance, no matter what time I arrive, I will completely unpack. I do not like the notion of "living out of a suitcase."

So, I will fill all of the dresser drawers with my socks, underwear, and casual clothes. I will hang up my suits, ties, and dress shirts. If I have flown, I will have to iron my shirts again. Judy has already starched and ironed them, but the suitcase wrinkles them again. Of course, the garment bag wrinkles my suits, but if you hang them on the shower rod and turn the hot shower on, the steam will take those wrinkles out in five minutes. After that is done, I put the shaving cream, deodorant, and toothpaste on the bathroom counter. My computer, sermon notes, Bible, and books all have their own entire specific place in my room. I spend so much time in hotel rooms that I have adapted my own routine, and I don't like anything to disrupt it.

But disruption is a good word to describe what happened in my hotel room one October evening in the state of Georgia. That is the night when I opened my door and was shocked to discover that somebody was in room!

Well, let me start at the beginning. I was staying in a beautiful hotel in the resort area of Brunswick, Georgia. One evening as I was leaving the revival service, a church staff member shared some information with me. He told me to be careful when I returned to my room each night. The brother cautioned me to park in a well-lit area of the parking lot as close to the door as I could get. I asked him why, and then he further enlightened me.

He told me about the scam that was going on in the hotel parking lots of that area. It seemed that hotel guests were being robbed as they were getting out of their cars. The thieves would hide in the dimly lit parking areas and then accost people as they walked to their room. Anyone wearing dress clothing and carrying a briefcase were prime targets. The thieves assumed that those people were in town on business, so they would have some money and credit cards on them.

Now, I really did not need to hear about this crime wave. First of all, ignorance is bliss. I am one of those fellows who don't need too much information. If I know about it, I might think about it. Second, I wear nice dress clothes every night! The robbers might think that I am a prosperous executive! They would have no idea that I am a poor evangelist!

I was wary that night as I parked my car. My head was on a swivel as I briskly walked to my room. Once I was safely locked in my room, I laughed about how silly it was to worry. I reasoned that I was in a secure hotel located in a secure area of the city. But twenty-four hours later, my attitude dramatically changed.

The next night, as I drove into the parking lot, I briefly thought about the story of the robberies. But I quickly dismissed those thoughts as I found a parking place in the most well-lit area of the lot. I emerged from my car with my arms loaded. The pastor had loaned me two or three of his study books. Someone had baked me a pecan pie, and I also had my Bible. I was trying to balance all of these things as I walked into lobby and headed straight for the elevator. Managing to free one finger, I pressed the button for the third floor.

When the elevator door opened, I stepped out and strolled down toward the end of the long hall. Amazingly, I had made it to my room without dropping anything, but I had to set everything down to open the door. I took that flat, plastic, room key out of my pocket. Then I reached down and loaded up my arms again. I did not want to leave anything out in the hall. I wasn't concerned about the thieves in the parking lot, but you just can't leave a pecan pie lying around! In one motion, I pushed in the key and burst into my room.

I usually leave a light on when I head out for the service. Tonight however, I had not done that. As soon as I walked into the room, the heavy door quickly closed behind me and left me in total darkness. Before I could reach for a light switch, I looked up – and there he was! Somebody was in my room. I stood right in front of him for a frozen moment. My heart was racing as I prepared to do battle. I dropped everything I was holding and got ready to charge. That is when I recognized my ugly intruder. It was me!

Swiftly I turned on the light and surveyed the scene before me. My room was a very nice room that included a spacious closet. The double-door closet was covered by an entire mirror. I had obviously gotten my coat out of the closet that night and failed to close the closet door. The half that was left open faced the entrance to my room. There were only a few feet between the two doors. Yes, I feel stupid talking about it now, but when you suddenly walk into a dark room and instantly come face to face with another person, it can be pretty unnerving. The most upsetting thing about the whole encounter was that I dropped my pecan pie – face down, on the floor!

To tell the truth, that same intruder who was in my room that night has given me problems before. To put it bluntly, I do battle with him all the time! He intrudes into my life at the most inopportune times. He wants to dominate me and defeat me. This relentless thief wants to overwhelm and overcome me. Now of course you know I am talking about me. That's right – sometimes I am my worst enemy. I am constantly fighting against my flesh. You probably have the same problem. Has it occurred to you that public enemy number one is the person you see in the mirror every morning?

Maybe you are thinking, "But isn't the devil my worst enemy?" Of course, the devil is the enemy of God and everyone who loves God. But our greatest fight is the one that we wage daily against our own flesh. Do you realize that we sin because we *want* to sin. Christians commit adultery because they *want* to. They look at pornography because they *want* to. They gossip, or cheat, or steal because they *want* to. In other words, their desire to please themselves is greater than their desire to please God.

Every Christian ought to memorize the words of the apostle Paul that are found in the book of Romans. *But put ye on the Lord Jesus Christ, and make not **provision** for the flesh, to fulfill the lusts thereof* (Romans 13:14). The word *provision* means, "don't make arrangements to sin." Go to great lengths to make sure that you aren't giving the flesh the opportunity to intrude.

I got excited that night in Georgia when I thought somebody was in my room. It is humorous to think about now. I mean, I almost attacked the mirror! But I will tell you something that is not funny. It is not funny when we let the one who is in the mirror attack us.

Chapter 13

Lights! Camera! Oops!

Proverbs 16:18 God says, *Pride goeth before destruction, and a haughty spirit before a fall.*

The Bible is the inerrant, infallible, inspired Word of God. Every single word of the Bible is absolute truth, and I can tell you from firsthand experience that if God says it, then God means it! He is telling the truth when He warns us that pride will knock us down. Unfortunately, I learned that valuable lesson the hard way.

The lesson came to me in my second year as a traveling evangelist. Up until that time I had been preaching in mostly smaller, rural churches. Now, as I look back over these years, I am grateful for the glorious opportunities that God has blessed me with. I never dreamed that I would be given the privilege to preach in some of the greatest churches in America. It has truly been a joy for a simple, country boy like me to get to preach in some of the places the Lord has put me in. Every day I thank Him for His gracious, bountiful blessings.

But I have also discovered that bigger is not always better. There are some big churches that are really small, and there are some smaller churches that are doing big ministries. I have often said that it is easier to preach to a hundred folks who have life, than it is to preach to a thousand folks who are dead. However, in those early days of evangelism I did not necessarily feel that way. I wanted to preach in the biggest churches, and that brings me back to the lesson that God painfully taught me.

I was invited to preach a revival at a large church in Tallahassee, Florida. At that time it was the largest church I had preached a revival in. The church had an attendance of about two thousand people. On top of that, they had a pretty big regional television ministry. Here I was, a young, struggling evangelist who was about to preach on television for the first time! This was the big break I had waited for. I just knew that my calendar was about to explode. Would you say that my priorities were a little mixed up? Let me tell you how silly I got.

The thought of television was so exciting that I became completely possessed by it. On Saturday night I stood in front of the mirror in my hotel room. I actually practiced my hand gestures and body movement. I surmised that I needed to preach with a little more class and dignity. Why, I even thought carefully about what color tie I would wear. I spent more time rehearsing than I did praying.

Sunday morning arrived and I awakened without an alarm clock or a wake-up call. Arriving at the church, I walked into the elaborate auditorium and admired its beauty. Then I spotted the television cameras at their various locations. As I recall, I thought about what place on the platform would be the best to do my Billy Graham impression. That would be the impression where I paused and put my hand over my mouth in deep thought. Listen, I know that you are probably amazed by this detailed and transparent confession. But I just want you to be aware of how messed up I was. Besides that, I am quite sure that you have been a bit prideful at one time or the other. Oh excuse me, I didn't mean to meddle. Let me get back to the story.

There is absolutely no question in my mind that our great God has a great sense of humor. After all, He watches us all the time. And we really do some dumb things. Also, I have no doubt that occasionally He gives us just enough rope to – you know! On this particular Sunday, the rope did not hang me. However, it did get all tangled up around my feet!

It happened right in the middle of my Sunday morning message. Here is an accurate and humiliating recap of the moment. The auditorium was filled with about two thousand people. The television cameras were rolling, and in my heart I am convinced the broadcast was being shown from coast to coast! I was working hard, trying to preach with passion and precision. I was wearing my best and most beautiful necktie. I was making a specific point to the television audience. As I walked across the platform, I never took my eyes off the camera. Suddenly, in midsentence I took a step forward. There was only one slight problem – I was already standing on the edge. So, when I stepped, I literally fell off the stage! The audience gasped as I tumbled off that platform and hit the ground with an agonizing thud!

My hip was hurting and so was my pride. That necktie that I was so concerned about was wrapped around my neck. And, at that moment all I could think about was a still, small voice deep in my heart. It was as if God was gently saying, "Rick, you keep looking at that camera, and I am going to knock you down again!" Well, I rose to my feet and assured everyone that I was all right. When the audience realized that I was going to live, a funny thing happened. They all broke out in hilarious laughter. Needless to say, all my dignity was gone.

As I look back over that embarrassing moment, I vividly remember learning two indelible lessons. First, I learned that the ministry is not a performance. The ministers who have the great privilege to stand on a public platform are not there to entertain or perform. Church is not a show. Preachers, teachers, and singers are accountable for what they do. They are also accountable for who they do it for.

In the last chapter we discussed the fight that all of us have with our flesh. We need to be very mindful about what God says concerning our egos. In 1 Corinthians 1:29 He tells us *That no flesh should glory in His presence.* God will not share His glory with anyone. We are living in the era of the Christian superstar. There are gospel singers today who perform instead of praise. And there are certainly preachers who preach for their glory and not His. All of us must constantly ask ourselves, "Why do we do what we do in the church?" Why do we teach, or lead, or give, or sing a solo? Why do we want our church to grow? Why do we want to baptize a lot of people?

Two verses later in 1 Corinthians 1:31, we are told *That, according as it is written, He that glorieth, let him glory in the Lord.* If God does not receive the glory for your ministry, then it is a mockery. Singer, you might be able to sing down the stars, but if you do not give glory to the Bright and Morning Star, it is a sham. Preacher, you might be able to really "shuck the corn," but if you do not give the glory to Christ, then it is only a show. The day that I hit the floor, God reminded me that He was the only One who was worthy to be lifted up!

The other important lesson that I learned that day has been a constant help to me over these years. Actually, it has been a source of liberation. I made the marvelous discovery that I didn't need to practice my Billy Graham impersonation. God already made the real Billy Graham, and God doesn't want an imitation; He wants the real thing. I found out that I could not be anyone else even if I tried. My name is not Billy Graham, or Jerry Vines, or Jerry Falwell. God never called me to be them. God has called me to be me. He has chosen to use me. He has uniquely designed and equipped me with specific gifts and abilities. There are certain things that I cannot do, and the great news is this: God does not expect me to do them! He does expect me to exalt Him by letting Him use me. God wants me to be the best me that I can be, and all of it is to be done for His glory and His glory alone!

Of course, God expects the same thing out of you. He expects no more, and He will accept no less. God has gifted you to do only what you can do. Your Father will not judge you based on what you cannot do. But you can be certain that you will be judged on the basis of what you can do.

So, let's all remember what this is all about – it's about

Jesus. We don't serve for the accolades and applause. We don't work for position or promotion. And we certainly don't minister for the compliments or the cameras. If you are doing it for you, then I can promise you one thing – sooner or later, God will knock you down!

Chapter 14

Power

Autumn is my favorite time of the year. There are many reasons for it. The air is crisp, and people seem more energized; it is a good season of the year for revivals. I enjoy sports and October has football and the World Series. But another reason I love the fall of the year is because of the colors of the trees. I preach many revivals in the mountain areas of the country, so I often get to see the magnificent kaleidoscope of colors. When all of those trees turn red, yellow, and orange, it is truly spectacular. It is always a real treat to see those gorgeous trees before the leaves begin to fall off.

Of course, we have beautiful trees in Florida, too, and there are a few that will change colors, but Florida does not have the fall splendor of the mountains. However, we do have fall in Ocala, Florida; fall does not usually arrive until about early December, and it will last until February. For about three months our trees will drop their leaves.

God has blessed us with a beautiful home in Ocala.

There are about twenty-five or thirty trees in our front and backyards. We have oak trees, dogwood trees, redbud trees, cedar trees, and good old pine trees. I like all of my trees, except when the leaves begin to fall. The leaves in my yard are not pretty. Instead, they are brown and ugly, and they cover up my driveway and front lawn like a thick blanket. If it rains on them, they make everything messy and filthy. So, for about three months of the year, I have to diligently keep my lawn raked.

Generally speaking, I like working in my yard. Both Judy and I spend a lot of time and energy trying to keep our grass, shrubs, and flowers looking nice. But I have to honestly admit that I absolutely detest raking the leaves, and I really hate it when the pine needles start to drop. Pine needles can be a particular nuisance because they cling to everything. Why, I have left home with one thin pine needle stuck to the windshield wiper of my car. I traveled a hundred miles at 70 miles per hour, and when I arrived at my destination, that pine needle was still there! Pine needles are tough! They look good when they are up in the tree, but when they fall on my driveway and the sap sticks to your shoes, there is a problem. Then, when the fallen leaves and pine needles mingle together, it doesn't take long for a nice yard to look nasty.

So, since I am the man of the house, it is my responsibility to clean up the yard. There are some things that just have to be done, and when I have to, I will do it. I will dutifully put on my gloves, grab the rake and wheelbarrow, and get out there and rake the leaves and needles. Of course, you understand that I am not the least bit happy about it. And most of the time I am griping while

I am doing it. Like a big baby, I will stand there and rake and mutter.

My wife thinks it is particularly funny when leaves fall while I am in the process of raking. I remember one time when I was out there raking my heart out. I was working hard trying to get all those leaves piled up. Suddenly a gust of wind blew through the trees. It seemed as if at least a hundred more leaves gently glided down to the ground and joined the ones that I was trying to rake up. When that happened, I looked up, and there was Judy. She was looking out the window and laughing. I just looked at her and smiled. I was so glad that I could bring a little entertainment into her day. So I just stood there with a sheepish grin on my face, and while I was grinning, I was griping about the stupid job that I had to finish.

But I want to tell you about the glad day when the griping finally stopped. One glorious Christmas morning I opened a present from my sweet wife. She had gotten me a Craftsman gas powered blower! The instructions said that it would blow with a force of 200 miles per hour!

I could hardly wait to get out in the yard. I excitedly mixed the gas and oil and poured it into the tank of my Craftsman 200 mph gas blower. Then I pushed the throttle all the way to the picture of the bunny rabbit. With utter delight I mashed the choke on my Craftsman 200 mph gas blower. I pulled the cord and started that engine of my Craftsman 200 mph gas blower!

There is one thing that I probably need to explain. I am a preacher of the gospel of Jesus Christ. That is about all I can do. Many preachers are multifaceted. They can work on plumbing, string electrical wire, or even do mechanical work. But my hands were made to hold a Bible. However, I am a power tool junkie. I love to hold a power tool, and every time I get a new power tool, it is a banner day for me.

One day Judy bought me a brand new gas powered edger. After I used it, I hung it up in the garage. I have a wonderful son-in-law whose name is Bryan Carter. That evening he and my daughter Rachel stopped by the house for a visit. Well, I immediately took Bryan to the garage and proudly showed him my new edger. When he saw it hanging there, he smiled and said, "I am surprised you don't have it hanging over the mantle!" Bryan knows about my love for power tools.

So you can imagine how thrilled I was to attack those leaves with my Craftsman 200 mph gas blower. I walked all over that front yard blowing leaves and pine needles. There was not a back-bending rake in sight. That blower did the job in a relatively short period of time. Really, I was kind of sad when I finished. I stood there for a few minutes and waited for the wind to start blowing some more leaves down! When it didn't happen, I was mildly disappointed! As I put my Craftsman 200 mph gas blower up, a sweet thought suddenly crossed my mind. I remembered how much I hated the job of cleaning up the leaves. It seemed to always be a hassle and a chore. It was amazing how much fun the job had suddenly become; it really wasn't much of a chore once I had the power!

The same thing is true in our work for the Lord. There are so many people who are unhappy with their service and ministry. Many only work in the church because of a sense of duty and responsibility. They never seem to have any joy or fulfillment in what they do. Their work is drudgery and misery.

There are even many men of God who appear to work more out of obligation than overflow. A wise man once said, "The most boring work in the world is church work when it is done without the power of God!" How true that statement is.

In Acts 1:8 Jesus Christ promised, *But ye shall receive power.* Our Lord gave us a big task to do, but He gave us big power to do it with. The work of the Lord is not easy work, and when any Christian tries to do it alone, it becomes frustrating. That is when it leads us to gripe and complain.

I can tell when I am anointed, but I can also tell when I am not. The Bible commands, *And be not drunk with wine, wherein is excess, but be ye filled with the Spirit* (Ephesians 5:18). There is one baptism of the Holy Ghost, and I believe that the Scriptures teach that we receive that at salvation. But there are many fillings. Those are the occasions when the Spirit of God fills us for the task at hand. Every evangelist, missionary, pastor, staff member, teacher, singer, leader, and worker should never try to do the work of God without the power of God. He gives us the power tool we will need for the specific tasks He wants us to do. It is time to quit using a rake; it is time to rely on the power of the wind!

Chapter 15

An Encouraging Word

There is nothing glamorous about the life of a traveling evangelist. Anybody who thinks so certainly has the wrong perception. Several years ago a young preacher told me that he wanted to be an evangelist. When I asked him why, he replied, "Because an evangelist doesn't have the headaches of a pastor."

Before I could respond, the brother continued by saying, "Also, evangelists get to stay and eat at the best places. And people really seem to admire full-time evangelists." In a very kind way I tried to explain to the young man that he was clueless.

There is a side to traveling evangelism that no one ever sees. The exhausting travel, the lonely rooms, the late driving, the early wake-up calls, and the heavy suitcases are just the tip of the iceberg. There is also the heartache of missing big events in the lives of my children. Coupled with that is the void that I feel because I am separated from my wife.

Yet, in spite of all of that, there is one thing worse than all of the others. It is the utter futility of being in a church that does not seem to care about revival. That is when the devil really jumps on me. He will tell me that I have sacrificed my family for nothing. He never stops there, and he won't stop until he has strategically attacked my calling, my ministry, and my commitment.

One time I preached a revival in the First Baptist Church of a small county seat town in Tennessee. We were having an attendance of about three hundred people nightly. But I want you to know that the services were graveyard dead.

The music was highbrow, the atmosphere was dry, and the environment was stale. The congregation gave no verbal affirmation whatsoever. They did not laugh, or shout, or grunt, or even burp!

During the very first service, I saw something that should have indicated what I could suspect that week. While I was preaching, I looked down and saw something incredible. The church organist was sitting on the front row, and she was reading something. What she was reading certainly wasn't the Bible. She was brazenly sitting there and casually thumbing through the colorful Wal-Mart advertising section of the Sunday paper! I was absolutely stunned. Here I was preaching my guts out, and she was checking the bargains at Wally World.

I was so appalled that I almost lost my composure. I stood in front of her and just kept preaching, and, of course, she just kept right on reading. Now understand, she was not holding the paper discreetly down in her lap. Oh, no, my friend! She was holding it up at eye level and demonstrating to all of those around her that she was more interested in the paper than she was the preaching.

Naturally, it upset me that she was disregarding my message and my preaching. Every preacher wants people to listen while he preaches. But what really grieved my heart was her apparent coldness concerning the Word of God. I must confess that I was angry, and I may as well tell you that I had a bad attitude. The truth is that I wanted to retaliate. I am ashamed to admit that I had a terrible thought. You see, occasionally I will expectorate a little saliva when I preach. That simply means that I can't help it, but sometimes I spit! Well, at that moment I wanted to spit on her paper. I wanted to lob a small missile and land it right between the *L* and the *M* of Wal-Mart. Though I tried, at that exact moment I couldn't work one up! In retrospect, I am glad that I did not spit.

After the morning service, I spoke to the pastor about his church organist. He assured me that she was no respecter of persons. He told me that she read something every single week he was preaching too. When I asked him why she was playing the organ in the first place, he told me that she was the only organist in the church. I kindly suggested to him that it would be better to have no one play at all than to have someone with an apparent attitude of disinterest. But he did not see it that way. So she just kept on playing for the worship service. Then she sat down, made herself comfortable, and opened up her reading material. During that revival week, she brought a variety of books to church. In the Tuesday night service, she read a *People* magazine. It became very frustrating to preach each night with that woman right in front of me. Satan was really using the situation to hinder me.

But the well-read organist was just part of the problem. The revival services themselves were totally cold and uninspiring, and the congregation seemed so unhappy and unfriendly. All in all, it was probably the most difficult church that I had ever preached in.

I was really becoming discouraged. Each night that I called Judy, I complained to her about the dead church I was at. I was heartbroken, homesick, and hurting. I felt like I was spinning my wheels. No one seemed to be listening, and I had a horrible feeling of uselessness.

Just before the last service began on Wednesday evening, something wonderful took place. It was about ten minutes before we began, and I was quietly sitting on the front pew. I was looking over my text for the evening. Quite honestly, I was happy that this particular engagement was almost over. I could not remember when I had spent a more defeating and draining week. In my heart, I really felt like it would have been better for me to have been home and resting all week.

At that very moment a man approached me and asked if he could speak to me. The man sat down and said, "Brother Rick, I know that this has not been an easy week for you, but I want you to know that your ministry has not been in vain." Then the gentlemen looked at me, and his eyes were glistening with tears. He continued, "You were sent here for me and my family this week. There is no way I can describe to you what God has done in our home these past few days. We were on the verge of disaster." Now, he did not tell me what the impending disaster was, but I could tell by the way he squeezed my hand that God had done something powerful in his life. As he got up to leave, he just kept repeating, "Thank you, thank you."

The man walked away, and I just sat there in wonderment. My first thought was, "Lord, I didn't think anyone was hearing anything this week." It was at that moment that the Spirit of God began to pierce my heart. It was as if my heavenly Father was sitting right next to me on that front row. He gently reminded me of my responsibility. Deep inside I felt as if God were saying, "Rick, you have allowed your anger at the organist to affect you this week." As usual, my Father was speaking the truth.

Because of my pride, I had lost my focus and my desire. I was wounded because one person did not want to listen, and it had affected my attitude about the entire church. Yes, they appeared to be an unfriendly congregation. But then again, so was I. All week long I had been aloof, terse, and cold. I had not wanted to be involved with anyone because one person had rejected me.

God continued to work me over, and I needed to hear everything He was saying. He reminded me, "You cannot make people like you or listen to you. You have one responsibility. I have called you to be faithful to preach the Book. Not everyone is going to receive it, but that is not your problem."

As the choir was walking in, I realized how unprepared I had been to preach that week. Because I was mad and wanting to get it all over with, I had spent very little time in prayer. I had discounted the church and had already written it off as a bad revival. Quietly, I bowed my head and asked God to forgive me. I confessed to Him that I was amazed that He had used me at all during that week. I praised Him for what He had done in the life of that precious family. Then, I asked Him to use me that night.

When it came time to preach, I was a different preacher that night. For the first time all week, I could not tell you what that organist was reading! I did not even look at her. Do you know what God did? He showed up – that's what He did! Souls were saved that night! For the first time all week, there was a spirit of buoyancy, freedom, and life.

The next morning as I was flying homeward, I thought about that man who had spoken to me on the previous evening. It was evident that God had greatly used him to encourage me. The sweet brother had just spoken a few brief words to me. Our conversation had probably lasted no more than two or three minutes, but he had spoken to me with such humility and sincerity. His words had brought refreshment, rejoicing, and even repentance in my heart! Thankfully, he had been obedient to God and delivered the message of encouragement.

More Christians should be sensitive to the voice of the Spirit and be encouragers. A simple word of encouragement is such a vital ministry to the body of Christ. In the book of Deuteronomy God told Moses to give a word of encouragement to Joshua. *But charge Joshua, and encourage him, and strengthen him: for he shall go over before this people, and he shall cause them to inherit the land which thou shalt see* (Deuteronomy 3:28). The word *encouragement* that is used in that verse is a strong word. It means "to fortify or buildup." God was not going to allow Moses to go into Canaan. Joshua was about to assume leadership, and God wanted Moses to be the one to encourage Joshua.

There are so many ways we can be used to encourage someone else. A phone call, an email, a timely card, or letter can be such an encouragement to a struggling believer. My wife Judy is a great example of that. She will occasionally put a sweet card in my suitcase. Once I was going through a tough stretch of meetings. I had not been in just one dead church, but there had been three or four in a row. Late on Saturday night I arrived at the destination of my next revival. I had been on a long flight and was physically weary as I began to unpack my suitcase. As I took my shirts out, I saw a card from Judy. Inside were the sweetest, most encouraging words. But the one sentence that blessed me the most simply said, "Keep on doing what you do. You do make a difference, Love, Judy."

Is there someone on your heart or mind today? Perhaps God is going to use you to encourage them. Please don't delay your intentions. Do it as soon as you can. In the name of Jesus, give an encouraging word.

Chapter 16

I Miss My Children

Lo, children are a heritage of the Lord:
and the fruit of the womb is his reward.
(Psalm 127:3)

"Daddy, I miss you and I want you to come home!" That desperate little voice on the telephone belonged to my seven-year-old daughter Jessica. I had only been a traveling evangelist for about two years. Jessie was having a hard time adjusting to Daddy being gone. Now, Jess was having a bit of a childhood crisis, and she wanted her daddy right now. The only problem was that I was hundreds of miles from home in a revival meeting. So, I prayed with my precious little girl over the telephone. I reminded her how much I missed her; then I assured her that I would soon be home. After we finished, I hung up the phone and wept for my child. I surely did wish I were home, but since I wasn't, I bowed my head and asked God to strengthen her little heart.

When my oldest daughter Rachel started the sixth grade, she was having a difficult time. Suddenly she was in a different school, surrounded by different people. Some her best friends from elementary school were not there, and she felt all alone. On top of all of that, Daddy was not there every morning to drive her to school. I knew she was lonely and blue, so I called her from my hotel room and prayed with her over the phone. I prayed that God would protect her all day, and I gently reminded her that her big God would watch over her in that big school. Before I had finished, both of us were crying. As I laid the phone back on its cradle, I was hurting that I could not be there to hug my girl. I sure did miss her, but I couldn't be there, so I got on my knees in my hotel room and prayed for her.

My son Jonathan was born on a Saturday afternoon. I held him, kissed him goodbye, and got on a jet to fly to New Orleans, Louisiana. As Jonathan has grown up, he has gotten used to telling Daddy goodbye. His daddy has been traveling since the day of his birth. We talk a lot on the cell phone. I have called him from the parking lot of a church to see how a ballgame turned out. There have been moments when I could not be there to cheer from the bleachers, but I have cheered him on from the phone. I sure do miss it when I can't see my son play, but I always pray for him and trust that he understands why Dad is not always around.

When Jonathan was very small, he would occasionally travel with me to some revivals. He was on airplanes before he was two years old. We always had a great time together, and he thought it was a big deal to stay in hotels and eat out in restaurants. The year before my son started school, he went with me quite often.

Neither he nor I realized how much we would miss each other once he had to go to school. I remember something funny that happened during the Christmas holidays after Jonathan's first few months of school. He had missed traveling with me during that fall. It was right before New Year's Day when my five-year-old boy decided to have a heart-to-heart talk with me.

I was relaxing alone in the living room watching a football game on television. Jonathan was in his room, playing with some toys that he had received for Christmas. About that time he strolled into the living room. Now, he wasn't old enough to really be interested in watching a ballgame, but he sat down in a reclining chair and gazed at the television. I watched him sit back and clasp his hands together behind his head. Like a little man, he crossed his legs and sort of cut his eyes over in my direction. He would look at me for a second or two; then his eyes would quickly dart in the other direction. I suppose it was cruel to let him suffer for a few minutes, because I could tell something real important was on his mind.

Finally, the little guy took a deep breath and looked right at me. I had let him suffer long enough, so I opened the discussion. I said, "Hey buddy, do you need something."

Deep in thought, he folded his arms. Suddenly he blurted, "Dad, I been thinking. I really need to quit school and travel with you!"

If I had not started smiling, I probably would have cried. I knew how much I had missed him, but now it was evident how his young life had changed. There he sat, wearing his little boots, children's dungarees, and flannel shirt, but he had made the monumental decision to be a kindergarten dropout!

Well, I knew this was a real delicate moment, and I needed to be careful how I responded. Though I may have been smiling, my small son was very serious. This was no joke. He knew school was about to start again, and he had no intention of going back. He was going to give up his education for life on the road. I looked over at his face. It was one of sincerity and determination. Now, he solemnly stared at me and waited for my decision to his proposal.

I slowly rose from the sofa, picked up the remote control, and turned off the game. I walked over to Jonathan and lifted him up. As I sat down in the recliner, I held him in my lap. I hugged him and reminded him how much I loved him. I shared with him how I had missed him traveling with me. I told him that my hotel room sure had been lonely without his presence. Then I looked deeply into his sweet, innocent eyes. He was waiting for my answer. I knew this was going to take some carefully worded, fatherly wisdom. Pausing for a moment, I deliberately chose my words. I said, "Son, I am sorry. But you can't quit school."

Then he looked firmly up into my face and whined, "But, why not?"

As I gazed back into his eyes, I said, "Because Son, your mother won't let you!"

* * * *

When Jonathan was about twenty-two months old, he went with me on an airplane to North Carolina. At that time he was allowed to sit on my lap with the belt buckled around us both.

There was a man sitting by us. As Jonathan squirmed in my lap, the man asked, "Are you a single parent?" I told the man that I was a happily married preacher. He was totally shocked and could not understand why I was going through the "hassle" of having my young son with me. He assured me that Jonathan was going to be a handful. He also predicted that this would be my last trip with him. The more he lamented about how my little boy was going to be an inconvenience, the more I quietly seethed. He talked about how glad he was that his children were finally grown. I was sick of his negativity, and I was just about to suggest that he "Shut up in the name of Jesus."

About that moment, Jonathan reached over and spilled my cup of Sprite. I caught the cup before it completely turned over. However, before I could, a few drops spilled on the man's trousers. Of course I profusely apologized. But as I turned away to the window, I clutched my boy and silently whispered, "Way to go!" Now, I would never allow my children to be rude to an adult, and I knew that Jonathan would not remember. But he could not have picked a better moment to spill a drink!

That first revival meeting with Jonathan was memorable indeed. When we got to North Carolina, we had a great time. Yes, he was very young. And yes, that meant that I had to bathe him, feed him, and dress him, but it was a pleasure just to have him with me. One evening during the revival, there was a church-wide, covered-dish dinner. I always like those meals. We Baptists are notorious for eating, and this was one of those spreads that had absolutely everything.

Well, I fixed Jonathan's plate, put him in his highchair, and tied his bib around his neck. As I was cutting up his food, a young father walked over to me. I really believe that he was joking when he said, "Brother Rick, you sure aren't helping us dads. When our wives see this, they are going to expect us to do it for our kids." I just politely smiled at him.

But a precious grandmother did not. An elderly woman overheard him speak to me. Boy, did she ever tear into him! She turned that boy every way but loose. She loudly explained to him what his responsibilities as a father were. This lovely granny read him the riot act. She preached him a message that almost had three points and a poem. She finished with her sermon, and several around her hollered "amen!" I thought they might give her a standing ovation, or at least take up a love offering!

The young father who had caused all of the commotion just turned red and tried to apologize. I did feel a bit sorry for him, but he really did ask for it. Anyway, when it was all over, I leaned over to Jonathan and said, "Buddy, you sure are stirring things up on this trip!" It sure was good to have him with me.

* * * *

Rachel was nine when I left the pastorate to enter vocational evangelism. Jessica was only five. Fourteen months after Judy and I surrendered to evangelism, Jonathan was born. This is not an ideal era for children to survive with a dad who is gone most of the time. But I am grateful to God that our children have survived. The truth is that God did not call my children into vocational evangelism. He called Judy and me into it. My children had to come along for the ride, but they have never displayed bitterness. And in addition to that, they have all been a vital and helpful part of our ministry.

I believe there are several reasons for that. First of all, my God is faithful. He is the one who called me, and He has graciously bestowed His goodness and grace to our family. Our great Father has met our every need. He has faithfully supplied us financially, physically, emotionally, and spiritually.

Another big reason that our family has survived is because of Judy. She is an extraordinary woman of God. She faithfully accepted our call into evangelism, and she has never backed up. She diligently keeps the home fires burning. Judy has to be the cook, cleaner, chauffeur, counselor, coach, consoler, and carpenter in the Coram house most of the time. Of course, everybody who knows us knows that Judy can fix most anything better than me! And she has done it with grace and grit. What a woman!

But there is one other thing I want to mention. Our family has had to learn to make each moment count. Because our time together is so brief, little things have become very significant. I'm talking about the real little things that we never really thought of as being all that important. Little things such as fifteen or twenty minutes of pitch and catch in the backyard. Hey, our family even gets a kick out of just sitting outside and watching our two killer dachshunds chase squirrels up the trees. We have learned to embrace and enjoy some of the simple moments in life that we once took for granted – things like just hanging out, renting a decent movie, or playing a board game together. Our family has tried to maximize our minutes, and God has helped us make the most of it, because after I went on the road, I quickly discovered how much I miss my children.

In Psalm 127:5 the Word says, *Happy is the man that hath his quiver full of them* [children]: *they shall not be ashamed, but they shall speak with the enemies in the gate.*

> *And if it seem evil unto you to serve the Lord, choose you this day whom ye will serve; whether the gods which your fathers served that were on the other side of the flood, or the gods of the Amorites, in whose land ye dwell: but as for me and my house, we will serve the Lord* (Joshua 24:15).

Chapter 17

Going Home

As I conclude this simple little book, I am writing yet another chapter from the seat of an airplane. I was not going to mention that, but something just occurred on my flight home. I am on a huge 767 Delta jet, and we are flying from Atlanta to Orlando.

It had been about fifteen minutes since takeoff, and I noticed that we seemed to be moving rather sluggishly. I was about to say that to the person sitting next to me when suddenly, the captain came on with a bit of disconcerting news. He said, "Good afternoon from the cockpit. We have turned around, and we are headed back to Atlanta. One of our wing flaps is not working, and we cannot climb any higher." As we looked around at one another, our captain continued. He told us, "We are going to take it as slow as we can, but when we hit the runway, we will be traveling much faster than is normal. Because of that, there will be crash equipment sitting near the runway. I will tell you more in a little while."

And with those few words, he abruptly signed off. The captain was very brief and businesslike, but there was nothing reassuring in his voice. You could tell that he was concerned about the landing. After a few more anxious minutes, he spoke to us again. The captain told us, "We are eight minutes from touchdown. Now ladies and gentlemen, as I said, we are coming in faster than we are supposed to, but we only have flaps working on one side of the plane. Fortunately, we have plenty of runway to work with. After we get it stopped, you will see fire trucks around the airplane. They will be inspecting the brakes to be sure they are not on fire."

The sweet senior lady next to me said, "Did he say fire?"

I replied, "Yes ma'am, that's what he said."

She nervously looked at me and said, "That don't sound good, does it?"

Then we heard the landing gear come down. The captain again quickly spoke, "Flight attendants prepare the cabin for arrival." I have flown enough to know that this was not the normal speed for a landing. It was a beautifully clear day. There was no bad weather or wind. But that mighty bird was shaking a bit as the buildings whisked by outside our window. Lower and lower we went until those wheels finally hit the runway. That jet kept on speeding, and you could hear the grind of the engines and the brakes.

When that 767 finally came to a stop, the applause began. It was some of the loudest cheering that I had ever heard on an airplane. One businessman was unmoved by the whole experience. He just sat there and hollered,

"What is everybody so happy about? We haven't gone anywhere!"

It is about an hour or so later, and they have put us on another plane. We are winging our way to Orlando. I have just turned my computer back on, and I am trying to put a finish on this book. I have thanked the Lord for giving me a good conclusion. Since I am on my way home, I want to close by talking about going home. Right at this moment, I am thinking about how good it will be to get home tonight. In fact, I should have already been home. I awakened this morning in Jackson, Mississippi. It has already been a long day, and I am anxious to get home. I know that the family has a big supper planned for me when I get home. And finally, I am on my way home.

One glad day all of us who are saved are going home! I just now thought about the little celebration we had a few minutes ago in Atlanta, Georgia. People were excited because our captain had expertly landed us safely. But one day every Christian is going to take the flight of the ages. And when the Captain of our Salvation sets us down on Beulah's shores, there will be a celebration. It won't be like that pitiful little exhibition on that airplane. Instead, it will be a concert of perfect praise that will last for the ages! And the focus of our praise will be on the One who has carried us there. We will forever praise the precious Lamb of God.

Have you ever thought about all of the things that we will celebrate in heaven? As I get a little older and my body gets a little more mileage, I am getting excited about a perfect body.

One year on New Year's Day, our family had a big

game of touch football. We called it the Coram Bowl, and we played it in the backyard. Here were the teams: On one team were my wife Judy (The most beautiful woman in the world, but she has no athletic ability), my sweet, pretty daughter Jessica (Jess is a cheerleader, she isn't going to break a nail or a sweat), and me! We were definitely the underdogs.

The other team was highly favored. They were my son-in-law Bryan (Who is a professional ballplayer and a great athlete), my son Jonathan (who is not a pro, but he is a good athlete – just ask him), and my daughter Rachel (Bryan's wife; she can actually catch a pass).

Now I ask you, is this a fair match up? No, it is certainly not. But I gathered my team together and gave them a big pep talk. We were all psyched up as we hit the field for the big game. Please understand that the game was just for fun, but if you are going to the trouble to play, then you need to play to win! I have a little competitive streak that runs through me, and I wanted a victory in the Coram Bowl!

Well, let me tell you what happened. My team came to play, and we gave it everything that we had. My wife Judy caught a touchdown pass! I publicly kissed her right on the mouth. I started to give her a high-five, but it just didn't seem like enough. Judy played great, and so did Jessie. She threw a touchdown pass! And so, late in the game, the score was tied 21-21.

It was starting to get late in the afternoon. Someone suggested that the next team to score would win the game. Bryan, Jonathan, and Rachel were really nervous. They thought they might actually lose to our inferior team. We drove the ball down the field (we were all the way past the rose bush), but we could not score.

Then it was their turn. Grimly, our defense buckled down to try to stop their great offense. It became obvious that Jonathan was going to throw the ball to Bryan. Rachel had played a good game, but Bryan is the athlete. If you just get the football near him, he will snare it with one hand. Now, I was the one who had to cover Bryan. When I was in school, the only real athletic ability that I had was in my legs. At one time I had a little speed, but those days are long gone, so I was trying to use my experience to cover Bryan. Simply put, that means that I was grabbing his shirt and holding him.

Now it was time for the moment of truth. Bryan took off and ran out for a long pass. He faked me out at the line of scrimmage, and I missed his shirt. He is very fast, and when he got behind me, I knew there was no way that I could catch him, but I was going to go down trying. As fast as I could, I sped up and chased him. My only hope was that Jonathan would under throw the pass. Then, at the last second, I looked back and saw Jonathan cock his arm to throw. While I was looking at Jonathan, I ran full speed, blindsided, into the oak tree in the backyard!

Thankfully, I did not hit my head. My right shoulder, side, and hip absorbed the shock. But I want you to know that it was a major jolt. The tree never moved, but I did. The collision instantly knocked me down and briefly took my breath away. My concerned family gathered around me. Jonathan was so concerned that he dropped the football and ran to my side. I could hear Bryan ask, "Brother Rick, are you okay?" Rachel and Judy were trying to administer aid to me. Everyone was really concerned except my wise cracking daughter Jessica. She looked down at me and asked, "Dad, how long has that tree been in the backyard?"

Laying there in intense agony, I suddenly had something to live for. I silently prayed, "God if you will help me get up, I will slap her!" But truthfully, her lighthearted spirit did cause me to smile. Then, when everyone saw that I was going to live, they started laughing.

Very slowly, I rose to my feet, and I limped into the house. I was so grateful that I wasn't hurt seriously. Nothing was broken or bleeding. Later, when I removed my shirt, my side was covered with an ugly greenish blue bruise. I winced when I saw that, but other than my neck being sore, I thought the worst was over.

That is until the next day when I tried to get out of bed. I absolutely could not move. My entire body throbbed and ached from head to toe. I felt like I had a cramp over my entire body. The tree had won and I lost. Painfully I inched to the side of the bed and rolled out. Every step was a chore. I was amazed that I felt as badly as I did. But the pain did not subside for almost a week.

Finally, one great day, I woke up and got out of bed. For the first time in nearly a week, I had no pain. I had forgotten how good it felt to feel good! I was reminded of some of my friends and family who never experience a day without pain. I know some people that are very close to me who do not remember what it is like not to hurt. As long as they live on this earth, they are going to have pain. Their world is one of prescriptions and pills, medicine and misery, doctors and disease.

Hallelujah, in Revelation 21:4 the Bible promises, *And God shall wipe away all tears from their eyes; and there shall be no more death, neither sorrow, nor crying, neither shall there be any more pain: for the former things are passed away.*

That word for *pain* literally means "anguish." Think about that for a moment. All of the things that cause us anguish will disappear. That includes all mental, emotional, and physical anguish. In the Old Testament it says, *For, behold I create new heavens, and a new earth: and the former shall not be remembered, nor come to mind* (Isaiah 65:17). God tells us that not only is He going to wipe away our tears, but He is also going to wipe away our thoughts. All anguish will be gone.

I was thinking about how wonderful heaven must be. Then I thought about all of the things in this world that bring us anguish. I got excited just imagining a world where those nasty things don't exist. So, I got out a piece of paper and started listing some of those things. Think about it, any bad thing that you can name from A to Z will not be in heaven.

A. Abortion will be abolished.
B. Beer will be banished.
C. Cancer will be cancelled.
D. Diabetes will be destroyed.
E. Evil will be eliminated.
F. Funerals will be finished.
G. Grief will be gone.
H. Homosexuality will be halted.
I. Indecency will be interrupted.

J. Jealousy will be junked.

K. Killing will be killed.

L. Lawlessness will be liquidated.

M. Mayhem will be missing.

N. Negativity will be negated.

O. Oppression will be over.

P. Pain will be past.

Q. Quarrels will be quieted.

R. Riots will be removed.

S. Storms will be stopped.

T. Terrorists will be terminated.

U. Undertakers will be unemployed.

V. Violence will be vanquished

W. Wars will be wasted.

X. X-Rays will be extinguished.

Y. Yearnings will be yesterday.

Z. Zero – As in zero taxes, mortgages, or baldness!

We are never going to remember any bad thing from this world. We won't remember the infections, injuries, or injustices of this world. We won't remember the tragedies, troubles, terrorists, or threats of this world. We won't be thinking about the Al Qaeda when we are worshipping El Shaddai!

I enjoy preaching revival meetings. I have the great privilege to meet some of the greatest people on the face of the earth. But no matter where I go, the best day of the week is the day I go home.

One of my fondest memories as a traveling evangelist is one of going home. I had preached a rare Friday night Bible Conference, and I was not home for our family night. My son Jonathan was only five or six years old at the time. He was ready for me to get home.

I was scheduled to fly out very early on a Saturday and get home by midmorning. Bad weather delayed my flight several hours. Then there was a mechanical problem that delayed me another hour or so. Consequently, by the time I got my car and drove home, it was late afternoon.

Yet, when I turned the corner, there was my little boy. He was sitting on his bicycle out in the driveway, and he was looking down the road for his daddy. When he saw that familiar car, he jumped off his bike and ran toward the house. He was screaming with joy, "Daddy is home, Daddy is home!" I had to stop and move the bicycle before I could pull into the driveway. At that moment my boy flew out of the garage with a grin on his face. He had dropped the bicycle and run inside to get the rest of the family. As we greeted each other, Judy told me, "Jonathan sat out here in the driveway all day. He's been looking for his daddy!"

One day Jesus is going to take us home. I want to be looking for Him with same expectancy my little boy looked for his daddy. Come quickly, Lord Jesus!

About the Author

Rick Coram, a full-time Southern Baptist Evangelist since 1988, accepted God's call to preach as a teenage boy. After college, he served for four years as a minister of students and for eight years as a senior pastor in two Baptist churches.

His last pastorate became one of Florida's strongest evangelistic churches, baptizing over 100 people per year for six consecutive years.

Since he entered traveling vocational evangelism, Rick has preached in over 1500 revivals, crusades, and camps. He is a frequent speaker at state and national evangelism conferences. RICK CORAM MINISTRIES is founder and sponsor of PowerLife Student Camps and the PowerLife Bible Conference. Since 1990, over 28,000 teenagers have attended the PowerLife Camps.

Rick, a native of Florida, makes his home in Jacksonville, Florida. He and his wife Judy have three children, Rachel Carter (husband Bryan), Jessica Turner (husband Patrick), and Jonathan Coram (wife Amanda). Rick and Judy have five grandchildren (Jadyn, Bralyn, Brooklyn, Ansley, and Gradyn).

Learn more about Rick Coram

www.rickcoramministries.com

Enjoy more titles by Rick Coram

https://www.rickcoramministries.com/books-ctl5

Good Morning God

How do you begin your morning? The way you begin your day has a significant impact on how the rest of your day goes. That is one reason why it is of utmost importance for a child of God to begin their day with God. In Psalm 5:3, David declared, *My voice shall you hear in the morning, Oh Lord.* David understood the importance of meeting the Lord in the morning. In Psalm 63:1, he said, *Oh God, early will I seek you.*

We are living in a volatile and vicious generation. Our enemy is attacking on every front. No Christian should ever consider leaving home until they have spent ample time with the Lord and armed themselves for spiritual battle. This daily devotional has been written to be a help for believers who want to spend time with their Father. Wake up each day and say "Good Morning God!"

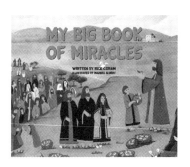

My Big Book of Miracles

An enjoyable, colorful book for children, *My Big Book of Miracles* brings to life creation, the birth and life of Jesus Christ, and each individual's need to personally experience the miracle of salvation.

The Return of King Jesus

One of the most recurring prophetic themes of Scripture is… Jesus Christ is coming – Jesus Christ has come – Jesus Christ is coming again! Just as sure as He came to the planet the first time, Jesus will return the second time. The first time He came to a cradle, wrapped in swaddling clothes. The next time He will come in the clouds, wrapped in robes of glory. The first time He came to be put in a graveyard. The next time He will empty the graveyards. The first time He came to establish His church. The next time He comes, He will evacuate the church.

The coming of our Lord should not be a surprise to anyone. The Bible is filled with wonderful promises and prophecies concerning the Second Coming. God does not expect His people to be eschatology scholars, but He does expect us to be diligent students of the Word. We need to be awake, aware, and alert. The event of the ages is at hand. It is almost time for…THE RETURN OF KING JESUS!